What's the Matter with Mommy?

Rantings of a Reluctant Stay-at-Home Mother

Kelley Cunningham

Wyatt-MacKenzie Publishing, Inc.
DEADWOOD, OREGON

What's the Matter with Mommy? Rantings of a Reluctant Stay-at-Home Mother

by Kelley Cunningham

ISBN: 1-932279-29-6
Library of Congress Control Number: 2006935774

Excerpts in this book have previously appeared in the following publications.

A monthly column "What's The Matter With Mommy?" on the webzine imperfectparent.com: Into the Abyss, I'm Down With OPK, If You Don't Finish your Kelp..., Please Don't Call Child Protection Services, WonderMom-ism: A Study in acceptance and recovery, Beautiful People Make Better Mothers, Between Menarche and Matriarch: Fashion's Death Zone, Dear Your Name Here, Happy Holidays!, The Screaming Trees: A Day's worth of school flyers, Mother's Little Cottage Industries, Quality Schmality, Zagat's for Parents, Back to school momku, Warped values, only 12.50 per child, cake included, How to be friends with a working mom, a primer

The Funny Times: Beautiful People make better mothers, Momku (shortened version), Keeping it Real, The Envelope please, Recipes for the Rest of Us, Just play nice with the other mommies

Brain, Child magazine: Zagat's for parents (shortened version), Hey Mom! What's in your stars?, The Envelope Please (shortened version)

Mamalicious magazine: Keeping it Real

EdgeCurve.com online 'zine: Zen Mama, Dieting the Mommy Way

The Mommyhood Diaries by Julie Watson Smith: The First full day of summer vacation

Published by The Mom-Writers Publishing Cooperative
Wyatt-MacKenzie Publishing, Inc., Deadwood, OR
www.WyMacPublishing.com (541) 964-3314

Requests for permission or further information should be addressed to:
Wyatt-MacKenzie Publishing, 15115 Highway 36,
Deadwood, Oregon 97430

Printed in the United States of America

Table of Contents

Introduction

There have been a ton of books lamenting the struggles of combining career and mothering, but for the most part us stay-at-home moms have been silent. We know that we are perceived as women who have it made, so we keep our mouths shut. Well, stay-at-home motherhood is not all Gummi Bears and Froot Loops, my friends.

If you decide to stay at home with your children you may feel as if someone pulled a lever and the floor has fallen out from under you, like some vaudevillian comic sketch. You are falling through a seemingly endless black tunnel that smells of the pediatrician's office. Here you are in another world you had no idea was co-existing alongside your old vision of reality. You may feel lonely, disoriented and terrified all in the space of a single diaper change.

Your working friends may think you're crazy to stay home. Gaping, Road Runner cartoon-like chasms emerge in many old friendships. Your own doubts can haunt you when the only feedback you get from your kids is a tearful "I hate you!" You most likely will become intimately familiar with the terms "double coupons," "consignment shops" and "Final Notice." You'll hear a lot of old ladies tell you to "cherish these days because they pass so quickly" as you fix a smile on your face.

Like a lot of women, I wound up as a stay-at home mother somewhat reluctantly after a disastrous series of attempts to combine motherhood and a career I had enjoyed. I tried everything: freelance, job-sharing, the "mommy-track," working from home, bringing the baby to work. By the time my first two children developed various issues that made it increasingly difficult for me to work, I was exhausted and mentally checked out.

One day, after explaining that my baby was sick again and I had to leave early to pick him up from day care, the boss laid into me. I quit right then. As I left the office for the last time, my heart thudding in my throat, I remember thinking … *what did I just get myself into?*

Suddenly, the next morning, I woke up and didn't have to go to work. I didn't know quite what to do with myself. I never thought I would be a stay-at-home mother.

I was horrified at putting down "homemaker" on forms when asked for an occupation. If I had dinner on the table when my husband walked in I felt slightly nauseated instead of proud. To say I had trouble adjusting was putting it mildly.

I was shocked at how lonely it is to stay home with babies. I felt like the freshman scrubs sitting on the bench: completely out of the game. How did our mothers do it? No wonder they had bridge clubs, Salems and really good diet pills. Anything to stave off the isolation and boredom.

I kept reminding myself that this was the best choice for my family at this point. But still, while the kids napped, I looked out my suburban front door at the tumbleweeds blowing by. I missed going out into the world. Look at all those people going places. I bet they had even brushed their teeth that morning. Surely they all must be headed somewhere fascinating, contributing profound knowledge to the world, or at least doing something which actually causes another person to hand them a check on a regular basis. And I couldn't even get around to throwing out the take-out Chinese cartons from last month that sat reeking in the fridge.

Being a reader, I looked around for support and all I could find were cloying parenting publications with cover babies who always seemed to be wearing sunhats. (Which just made me feel like more of a loser, since my kids always pulled off their hats.)

I read about moms who thrilled at another game of stack the blocks, were driven to tears of joyful wonder over their children's BM's, and worried way too much about the entertainment they should hire for their toddlers' birthday parties.

Was I the only one who cringed at this? Anyone else out there who owned up to some occasional mixed feelings about her decision to stay home? Wasn't there anyone else who often wanted to leave the kid on the corner with a FREE TO GOOD HOME sign around his neck?

After awhile it became clear that there are two types of stay-at-homes. Those who carry their toddlers' Cheerios around in custom-designed, mail-order caddies with "Cheerios" printed on them, and those who just keep re-filling the same, dusty Ziploc baggie. Those who are truly content and totally into it, and those who keep thinking "but I should be DOING something ... "

I stopped pretending that I was the former and started testing the waters. I'd throw out little jokes about the dubious joys of raising kids that hinted at a wee bit of trouble in paradise, just to see if anyone laughed. To my happy surprise, some did. All of a sudden I found a lot of other mothers who were also searching, edgy and tired of having to smile while being dubbed soccer moms.

We were all very conscious that staying at home was a luxury, even though most of us were struggling financially, so it was pretty ingrained in us not to complain. Most of us had read, or at least heard of, the current crop of Mommy books and were aware of the reviews opining we were the whiniest, most self-absorbed generation of mothers ever.

Well, I don't know about that. Maybe it's true, or maybe we just feel more inclined to voice the same feelings our grandmothers had, but didn't dare share. Everybody else in our society has the inalienable right to whine about their jobs. How come when us mothers (everyone knows we have the most demanding job of all) own up to a bit of a struggle, we are lambasted?

Strange. Is our society so short-sighted when it comes to motherhood? Once we give birth do we lose all other facets of our personalities? Are we all that conflicted? Why does every complaint have to start with a disclaimer? For instance: "I love my children, but I have the urge to hide from them every evening around dinnertime." We always have to throw in the "I love my children" bit. As if being honest about the difficulty meant we didn't.

We all love our kids more than our lives, alright? We're all not just a bunch of navel-gazing sissies who can't hack raising kids as well as the generations who came before us.

I decided to start writing about all these up-again, down-again feelings that staying home with my kids brought out in me. At first I kept the essays to myself, but after tentatively showing them to a few kindred-soul moms and getting rave reviews, I started submitting. To my surprise a lot of them were published. I was thrilled and flattered (and not a little bit shocked) to receive overwhelmingly positive feedback. Mostly along the lines of, "You really tell it like it is!"

So I collected some of my writing and put together this book.

It's a bit of support for all those so-called stay-at-home moms for whom playgroups look like a kind of death and believe "scrapbook" should never be used as a verb.

Every once in a while, there's nothing better than an honest-to-goodness, balls-out (for lack of a feminine equivalent) bitch session. I don't pretend to have any answers to the vexing questions regarding the changing nature of motherhood in today's world; I just need a good laugh.

Don't Even Bother: The Case Against Childbirth Preparation Classes

Do you feel that you were well prepared for childbirth? Were you able to distinguish the mucous plug from snot as you peered into the john for signs that labor was starting? Did you do your kegels while riding the subway to work, quite amazed that you could be doing something so intimate in such a public place while everyone around you was unaware? Did you pack a tennis ball in your hospital suitcase so your partner could rub your back with it, like I did for my first baby?

I'm betting that you had other ideas about what your partner could do with that tennis ball once the real pain hit.

Let's face it: childbirth preparation classes are a whole lot of hooey. Maybe we expect too much of them, because nothing can prepare you for the moment of ghastly realization that this kid is coming out and it's going to hurt like nothing ever has. And that you can't go home, have a glass of wine and forget the whole stupid idea. All the tidbits of advice they give you fly out the window, the first being the flipping tennis ball. It won't hurt to play the Enya CD, mama, but it certainly won't help.

My decidedly un-P.C. picture of childbirth preparation classes may seem harsh to glowing and clueless moms-to-be. But the truth is that they only offer these classes to give you something to do now that your feet have become too swollen for shoe shopping. What else is there to do now that you've ordered the crib and laundered all the newborn onesies in Dreft?

Back me up, all you experienced moms out there. Did you really bond more closely in the class with your husband as he sat behind you, legs akimbo? How oddly voyeuristic was it to watch all the other couples doing this? I sure as heck didn't want to go out for a romantic dinner afterwards. I just wanted to go home and try to forget the sight of the panting, obese woman next to me. The only conceivable (pardon the pun) purpose this experience may provide is to give you an idea of how many people are going to be looking up your yanni when you're spread-eagled on the delivery table.

Did your Lamaze instructor tell you to pinch your husband's hand progressively harder while he panted so he could sense how a contraction feels? What a helpful exercise! That's like trying to explain how a guillotine feels by giving somebody a haircut. Look, I'll never know what it feels like to get slammed in the nuts, and there's no way he will ever remotely understand what childbirth feels like.

God knows my husband tried his best as a labor coach, but maybe, just maybe, he didn't belong in the delivery room. He was way out of his league. (Hell, I was way out of my league!)

Perhaps we should at least give men the option to opt out. I wouldn't blame them. I would rather have been chain-smoking in the waiting room than sweating in the delivery room if I had had the choice.

Childbirth has been women's work since time immemorial and perhaps that's the way it was meant to be. I suppose I'm glad my husband could see his children being born, but this is a man who nearly passed out the first time because he forgot to eat for twelve hours. The second time he also forgot to eat and almost passed out when the OB asked him to cut the cord. The nurse had to help him into a chair while I'm pleading "hey...a little help here! I'm in a bit of pain!."

The third time he wisely got an Egg McDuffie and munched it while his third son came into the world. This is absolutely true, I swear. All the while chatting with my OB about going out for martinis. I need this? I'm trying to have a baby and I have to remind him to eat? I think the thing that fascinated him most was the contraction ticker-tape machine. He would kindly inform me that another one was coming up and boy oh boy it looks big!

I think the only thing more annoying would be a man who is way TOO involved. You know the type who says "we're pregnant!." No, Ding Dong, your wife is pregnant. Put away the camcorder and get her some ice chips, stat.

There was something romantic about the old days with the smoke-filled waiting rooms and the pacing fathers. The nurse throws open the swinging doors and says "Mr. Ricardo, you have a healthy son!" And he passes out anyway but at least I wouldn't have to deal with it. Then he gets to hand out cigars and get slapped on the back by all the other expectant fathers. Men need that bonding and they can't have it now that they're holding our knees next to our ears while we push.

I'm kind of like an animal when I'm sick or in pain. I want to be alone. Just let me crawl behind the sofa to die, thank you. Don't tell me how great I'm doing.

Like all earnest first-time moms, when I discovered I was pregnant I couldn't wait for the Lamaze classes to begin. I was planning on a natural delivery. No drugs for me. I can take pain!

I once ran a ten-mile road race with temperatures in the single digits. Thanks to a sadistic dentist I had a root canal with insufficient Novocain. I pierced my own ears after a few beers. I skied in minus-fifteen-degree weather until my nose was frostbitten. I drank a frat boy under the table in a shot contest. I am total chick macho. I can run with wolves. Women have been giving birth for millions of years and I can too!

Well, after pride cometh a fall, otherwise known as Pitocin. They cranked up the IV and I had a contraction that tore me in two. I thought for sure someone had disemboweled me but the nurse looked at the monitor, merely shrugged and said "Oh, that was a good one." At that point I knew the only way Enya would help is if she were the one having the baby instead of me.

When I started to panic and became convinced that I could not possibly climb this Everest in front to me, the nurses reminded me of all the helpful tips I learned in childbirth preparation class.

"Don't work against your body. Work WITH your body. Just go with it."

Are you talking to me? How can you tell I'm not working with my body? Is there some vital piece of body-awareness information that I'm missing? All I know is that this body I'm unfortunately inhabiting at the moment is in a bit of a quandary from trying to pass an ICBM missile through an opening which God in his infinite wisdom made absurdly inadequate for the purpose. Therefore, I am reacting with grimaces of pain contorting my face.

"It's good pain. It's pain with a purpose!"

Come over here so I can punch you in the jaw. That's pain with a purpose too.

"Take three quick breaths, then hold it and push!"

Push what?

"Don't grunt like that. You'll have a sore throat in the morning."

I'll be dead in the morning if there's a God in heaven.

"Channel that womb energy."

Huh?

I knew then that even the nurses thought it was all bullshit, but what else can they say? They have to talk you down off the ledge somehow. If they had said, "*Lady, you're on your own, believe it or not you'll get through this like everyone else,*" it wouldn't be very helpful. But at least it would be honest.

Maybe we should take Prissy's advice. In *Gone With the Wind* she wanted to put a knife under Melanie's bed to cut the pain in two. Why the hell not? It's as good an idea as any other.

Every mother remembers her babies' births until her last breath. I won't go into details about the nauseating narcotic haze, or waiting for the anesthesiologist to stop by after his coffee and gossip break to administer epidurals that didn't take or worked too well. The forceps. The episiotomies. The hemorrhaging. All I know is I got Shit Karma in the Wonderful Childbirth Experience department.

Whenever I relate my birth stories to Earthy-Crunchy Moms, they're convinced it was the episiotomy that made everything go south for me. They tell me if I had massaged my *moonachie* with organic cocoa butter an episiotomy would not have been necessary. Then I mention that my baby was nine pounds seven and they slink away horrified. No one's hoo-hah is that big and I daresay that even a Costco-sized vat of cocoa butter wouldn't have done the trick. Anyway, I wanted that baby out of me so badly I would not have cared if they sawed me in two to hasten the process.

Another admission that will further sully my chances of winning "Mother of the Year" is this: when the baby was finally born, I didn't cry with joy. I didn't yearn to hold him. I merely looked up to see if he was breathing and let my head fall back onto the bed. I was so utterly relieved that the agony was over that that's all I could think about. Oh, after a few moments I started to get curious about the tiny, slimy creature pooping on the french-fry warming tray, but only after it sunk in that I wasn't going to die.

Thank God we came through it. By some monumental lapse of reason I returned to the Maternity Pavilion twice more. I've got three wonderful sons, spider veins and a little stress incontinence to show for it all. Happy ending.

But when I hear about women who had unmedicated births in hot tubs, or how for them pushing wasn't anything like the excruciating hell I experienced, I start to twitch. *"It was such a relief to push!" "My focal point was a picture of my husband on the wall and before I knew it she was born!" "My Doula rubbed my back with a dong quai poultice, did a dance appealing to the moon goddess and fed me raspberry tea. It took all the pain away!"*

Well, I don't buy it for a minute. You are so full of shit. I don't like you, I don't trust you, and my kid is not going to play with your kids, you evil, Stepford-wife pods! Don't make me beat you about the head with my consignment shop-purchased Baby Bjorn.

Every few weeks there's another baby that just pops out in the cab on the way to the hospital. I love the stories of the women who go to the ER with a case of indigestion that turns out to be full-term twins. I have to say I just don't get it. It is absolutely incomprehensible to me.

Strangely, some of the women I know who have had the easiest labors are the biggest wusses with anything else. They couldn't run a block without getting winded but they breeze through labor without so much as a twinge.

God knows what I did in a past life that earned me the honor of being the Rotten Childbirth Poster Child in this one. Wait, I know. I was a childless Lamaze instructor. That's gotta be it.

Bring On Da Belly, Bring On Da Frump

Feeling sexy as you swallow that boulder they call a pre-natal vitamin? Feeling chic in your denim-like jumper? Don't those maternity undies put you in the mood for luv? No? You must be doing something wrong!

There's too much pressure nowadays to remain sexy and fashionable throughout pregnancy. Who needs it? That's what got us into this mess in the first place.

Pregnancy is not the time to look chic. Forget sexy. Waddling through pregnancy is hard enough. If your belly button has popped out, giving you the appearance of an overcooked Butterball, it means you're done.

For me, sex took a seat at the back of the minivan straightaway. Maybe it was a sign that the first time I did the pee-on-a-stick thing, I was in the ladies room at work. I wasn't awaiting the results with my husband beside me, curled up on the couch in front of a roaring fire. I think I had other things on my mind at that moment besides romance.

But besides the pressure to remain sexy, there is also a ton of pressure to stay stylish. The magazines are full of tips on how to dress attractively during pregnancy. Oh, forget it. I was one of those women who viewed pregnancy as the only time in my life when I wouldn't have to suck in my tummy at cocktail parties.

I say bring back the frumpy stuff, like those *I Love Lucy* big bow smocks and flats. Wearing heels during pregnancy should be a felony. Muumuus? Bring 'em on! There should be a maternity clothing store called "Husband's Shirts n' Leggings."

It doesn't help either that the tabloids are chock full of

pictures of pregnant celebrities who manage to keep looking great. Isn't it fun to see how cute Kate Hudson looked at eight months, while you resorted to wearing two-dollar flip-flops from CVS because it's the only thing that fit your huge, swollen flipper feet? I love how the celebs walk around in dresses so tight you can actually see the baby kick. I wonder how that would have gone over at my office.

In any case, I didn't have the budget to drop thousands at "Pea in the Pod" for a cute, sexy pregnancy wardrobe even if I had really cared about looking attractive. I begged, borrowed and stole from friends who were done having babies. Maybe I was too practical, but I thought, why spend the money on something I'm only going to wear for a few months? Okay, I wound up having two more pregnancies, but I didn't know that then.

Anyway, by the second and third go-around I really didn't have time to think about my looks. I was too busy spackling my first child's mouth with mashed peas. I would often forget I was pregnant, only to be continuously surprised by the watermelon I was carrying in front of me.

So fashion wasn't a big consideration. Comfort was. I think I wore the same dorky elastic-waist jeans (acid-washed!) throughout all of my pregnancies, until I finally split the crotch during a Lamaze breathing exercise class. I may have looked like a street person at times, but at least the dimes passers-by kept throwing me came in handy when it was time to buy the Diaper Genie.

Even as I entered my tenth (or was it fifteenth?) month the pressure to be sexy didn't let up. I was late with all my babies. People actually told me to have sex to bring on labor. Huh? Hell, no! I was peeing every ten minutes and squatting on the john, looking for signs of the elusive mucous plug. By that time my belly was so huge I needed a trampoline to vault into bed. That sort of killed the mood anyway.

So as a seasoned mother-of-three I'm here to say: there's life after pregnancy. Yes, stay healthy, but don't beat yourself up if you're not looking and feeling so hot. Savor this fleeting stage and don't sweat it now, sisters. Or at least, not any more sweating than the pregnancy is already bringing on.

Enjoy the frump stage! You can go back to your old body (well, almost) and your sexy clothes in time. I just won't mention that someday you will have to scoop up your post-nursing boobs and arrange them in a padded, push-up bra, but that's what those bras were made for.

Into the Abyss: Fear and Loathing on the Road to Preschool

It seems to me parents have enough to worry about these days without borrowing more anxiety. I am talking, of course, about preschool.

What is merely supposed to be an opportunity for the little darlings to break free of their sequestered plastic bubbles and interact with other creatures of the same height and lingering smell, sharing bacteria and ancient blocks (oops, I mean manipulatives), has now turned into yet another humorless migraine-inducing educational opportunity designed to take the fun out of raising kids once and for all.

The umbilical cord is still hanging on by a thread and you start hearing the dreaded phrase "Have you thought about preschools?" Hearing this question would give me the same rotten feeling in the pit of my stomach as when I used to hear 'so what are you going to do for a living?' when I announced I was majoring in art.

Not wanting my toothless genius to fall behind his peer group, I decided to investigate the local preschools. Check out some of these phrases from real-life ads for preschools in my area.

"Let us help your child develop an inner thirst for knowledge that will last a lifetime." That's a lot to expect from fingerpaint.

"Designed to meet each child's developmental needs and promote a positive, secure and accepting environment enabling each child to grow with a sense of joy and wonder." Wow. I kind of just want him to stop picking his nose.

"Favorable student:teacher ratio allows maximum individualization. Children are placed in three classes according to ability."

What abilities are they talking about? The ability to grab toys from your peers deftly or the ability to belch the ABC's?

"Our highest priority is the development of self-esteem, creativity, and love of learning. We provide a cumulative program with developmental goals for all ages." Jeez, I'm exhausted just reading this. We're talking about three-year olds, folks.

All of this sounds wonderfully well-meaning and lofty, but can we take a step back here? My kid's happy to keep his pants dry and they want to teach him irregular French verbs. At this stage it might be more important that kids learn to wash their hands after pooping than the properties of magnets, post-modern architecture and bebop jazz.

Of course, preschools advertise this way because parents have come to expect this kind of nonsense jargon, and they want the best for their kids. What parent would sign up for a preschool that tells it like it is? *"We'll keep your kid busy for two hours with some homemade Play-Doh so you can go home and pee by yourself for a change."* Well, I would, for one.

The registration process has become a quagmire of waiting lists, registration fees and politics. The first time I faced this I stupidly showed up with my child's birth certificate and a checkbook, and told my husband to wait in the car. My jaw dropped as I entered a sweltering room swarming with hundreds of parents, crying children, and a registrar with a bullhorn. A registrar? For preschool? The first time I heard the word "registrar" was my freshman year of college.

I've heard horror stories of some preschools actually interviewing the families and the prospective students. What in the hell can possibly be gleaned from an interview with a three-year-old? That race cars go really really fast zoom zoom zoom?

One would think from all this hysteria that the preschool a child attends determines his course for life. The whole idea of selecting just a few children to receive all the best, especially at so young an age, makes me want to throw up. How do they determine a suitable candidate from a gaggle of crotch-grabbing three-year olds? Is it something obvious, like one kid who breaks free from the crowd to perform a daring interpretation of "Clymenestra"? Or is the selection process more subtle? *"Let's see, we have to narrow this down. They're ALL scratching their tushies. But the first one who smells his fingers is OUT."*

I think it was different when we were kids. Did you even GO to preschool? If you did, wasn't it in a dingy church basement for four or five hours a week? Do you even remember it?

But that was then. Now, every decision parents make is fraught with worry. We're all nervously watching our children, paging through those stupid "What to Expect" books, making sure they are Hitting Their Developmental Milestones on time. Or, better yet, early. *"Look, little Jared is throwing sand at the other kids and he's only 18 months old! The book says that's really early to show such sociopathic behavior!"*

I think my kids are in big trouble. I purposely did not send them to the Best Preschool In Town (even though I suspect the only difference is that the sand table looks newer). I did this mainly because I couldn't stand the smug attitudes of the mothers who did. I didn't think I could tolerate making small talk with them every morning for two years.

Because of my selfish decision I fear I am dooming my darlings to a lifetime of menial jobs and shiftlessness. Oh well, I'd rather have a family discount at Burger King than a Phi Beta Kappa key that doesn't go with anything.

The competition starts early. Those of us who stay at home with our kids know that there are children who have been at day-care since they were six weeks old. By the age of three some of these prodigies are working their way though the Romantic poets and can distinguish between Baroque and Rococo. We think we HAVE to send our kids to preschool or else our little dullards will be doomed.

Yeah, yeah, I know a child's potential is limitless, and that these are the years where their little brains are like sponges and will absorb anything. Maybe I'm not expecting enough of my children. Maybe the primo preschool experience really does lead to a lifetime of awe-inspiring achievement, and to show-off parents who proudly slap that Princeton decal on the rear window. But what benefit is it to have a child who grows up to be a Rhodes scholar if he still is incapable of sharing the damn blocks?

I'm Down With OPK (Other Peoples' Kids)

How I wound up as the stay-at-home mom of three kids is still a wonder to me. That's what I get for having too much Merlot, an active imagination and *Last of the Mohicans* on video. It's a slippery slope from "Oh what the hell, Hawkeye, let's go for it" to "Goddammit how many times do I have to ask you to put your shoes on? We're late for school again!"

However we stumble upon it, Parenthood is a minefield we are all trying to negotiate without a map, and it's full of surprises. Among the many surprises for me is how much I have to deal with Other People's Kids (from here on referred to as OPK). Somehow when you're carrying home that bundle wrapped in a white flannel with the blue and pink stripes you pinched from the hospital, you don't see yourself six years down the road yelling at someone else's kid to stop at the corner.

No one tells you that you will be wiping OPKs' heinies, blowing OPKs' snotty noses, and holding OPKs' chewed wad of bubble gum in your hand.

I'm always in awe when I hear people talk about how much they love OPK. "Oh, I just had to be a teacher because I just LOVE working with kids." I admire these people like I admire people who have completed an Iron Man Triathalon or who don't curse. I'm glad these people exist as an inspiration to us, but I sure as hell ain't one of them. A woman's got to know her limitations.

The older your kids get the more you have to deal with OPK. The preschool playdates will evolve into an awkward interruption of a fumbling pre-teen make-out session with some pimply-faced skank on the moldy basement couch.

Like all parents, I have my share of OPK war stories. I remember the time my four-year-old had a friend from preschool over for a (God, I hate this term) "Playdate." This kid is already on my nerves on the car ride home because he doesn't just talk, HE TALKS LIKE OWEN MEANY ALL THE TIME. He's holding his nose the whole way because he says my car stinks.

Three hours later, after refusing what I made for lunch and spilling it, pissing himself twice and crying because my son wouldn't play with him (good for you, my boy) I was never so happy to see a kid go home as I was that day. These are the "play-dates" (wince) where the other mother is sure to ask, "How did it go?" And you have to lie like a rug.

Then there comes the time when your kid is getting terrorized at the playground (which has always been a field-study in natural selection on the best days) by a kid who's obviously been raised by wolves and most likely does not have opposable thumbs. You look around for the parent/caregiver/nanny/alpha dog to notice the situation and correct it. And there's no one. So what do you do? How far can you go? Are you limited to dirty looks or can you whip out the wooden spoon?

This is a situation where I defer to Darwin. My eyes narrow, the fur on the back of my neck stands up and it's survival of the fittest all the way. And guess what, kid. I'm still bigger than you. I'm higher up on the food chain. So stay away from my cub or you're going down faster than a sick wildebeest on *Wild Kingdom*.

Don't be shocked. You've been there. It's instinctive. Wait until the next time some little mongoose won't give your kid a turn on the swings. You take him aside and whisper in his ear. Give up the swing or I'll hang you by your ankles on the safely-padded, brightly-colored plastic monkey bars'.

But having said all this about OPK, I know I'm setting myself up for a fall. Any mother knows the second you say to yourself 'my kid may be rotten, but at least he doesn't pick his nose and eat it' you have instantly awakened the Parenting Gods. Soon, probably this very afternoon, your darling child will exhibit the exact behavior you found deplorable in OPK.

The Parenting Gods don't like moms who gloat or compare. I will pay. It's just a matter of time. So I beg forgiveness by stating that I know my kids are OPK to everyone else. I think the key here is awareness of that fact.

We all have to accept that our own kids can seem at times, well, downright annoying to everyone else. I've accepted this about my darlings and it is a freeing feeling. Hey, I've done my best, but my shoddy parenting skills are as obvious as everyone else's.

So please feel free to tell my kid to stop pestering your toddler and to share the toys. If my kid is being rotten then I want someone to tell him so. I don't care who it is. Heck, he's probably more inclined to listen to someone else anyway.

Some mothers get very territorial about that, though. "I'll discipline my own child, thank you very much." OK, lady, whatever, but why don't you try it sometime? *Now* might be good, because as we debate this issue the fruit of your loins is kicking my child in the head.

Does it or does it not take a village? Pick one and let's go with it. I just wish I didn't live in the same village as that kid who thinks my car stinks.

If You Don't Finish Your Kelp, You Can't Have Any Acidophilus!

Please save us from the earnest Organic Moms. You know the type. They show up at the preschool party with tofu and seaweed muffins while the best you could do is slice and bake chemical tube cookies. They have lots of instructions for playdates too. *"Please don't give little Logan any juice because kids who drink juice don't grow tall, no gluten because he has onomatopoeia, and keep in mind he may not eat your grape jelly because he's used to homemade."* Guess what Logan does when he's at my house. Begs for the store-brand sandwich cookies while zoning out on Bugs Bunny. Secretly, I enjoy this. Have some more processed nuggets, Little Lord Fauntleroy.

I would admire these mothers' good intentions if only they would keep their superiority to themselves. But when they roll their eyes at the moms who could only manage to bring in Oreo's for the pre-school snack I get an urge to shove some Cool-whip into their gobs.

You would expect their children to have an aura of healthy wonderfulness about them. The light reflecting off their children's *Tom's of Maine*-cleansed teeth would blind the rest of us. The funny thing is their chemically-challenged kids don't seem any healthier than my chemically-enhanced children. They have just as many hacking coughs that you try to pretend you didn't notice before school drop-off time. (Gosh, he *seemed* fine this morning.)

Maybe I'm just jealous. There's no way I have the discipline to research every morsel my child eats. I'm too lazy. Especially when they keep changing the rules midgame. You think you have it nailed until you find out the formerly wholesome snack food you've been serving up is loaded with not just fat, but THE WORST KIND OF FAT.

Also, I don't have the money. Apparently better health is reserved for the trust fund babies. Side by side sits the regular broccoli and the organic broccoli. At twice the price it's really hard for me to justify buying the organic. I figure I'll just rinse it a little more and hope for the best. "But if you buy organic it's better for the planet" say the Organic Moms as they pull out of the Whole Foods parking lot in their Yukon Denalis.

I guess it's that lack of consistency that vexes me. Will it behoove my family to eat soynuts all day while we're stuck in traffic behind a toxin-spewing Mack truck? Will the fish-oil capsules I swallow protect me from the mercury in my dolphin-safe tuna salad? There's just no way one can be completely pure and clean, living as we do on an imperfect, festering planet. I suppose you have to at least try, but don't beat yourself up if your kid occasionally eats a maraschino cherry instead of a Kale Krunchie Bomb.

Not that I'm letting Big Food off the hook, mind you. I know what they're trying to do to us: make us buy more food. And they're trying to do it at a profit by using less than the best ingredients. This shouldn't be a news flash. It's big business. It's evil. But does that mean we have to chuck it all, get a land claim in Alaska, and live on bark and berries? I mean, maybe you can have a Pop-Tart every so often. I think the trouble starts when you start going through a case a week. And besides, you can't tell me the Organic Moms aren't raiding the cabinet looking for Brown Sugar Cinnamon Pop-Tarts after they've indulged in a satisfying, post-PTA meeting spliff. Or so I've been told.

I suppose it is indicative of our culture. If a little is good then more must be better. That mentality trickles down to the health front. It's not enough to cut down on your kid's Cheeto consumption and force-feed them some broccoli every few weeks. No, you must go completely organic and make sure little Morgan eats only soy-based protein and organic pine-nuts. I mean, I like hummus as much as the next person, maybe more, but if you can resist Cheeze Doodles then I don't trust you.

Perhaps Cheeze Doodle consumption will soon be regulated for our own good, just as smoking has become a criminal act. I used to smoke and I must say I really liked it. I know quitting was the right thing to do but I refuse to brand all smokers as weak, pathetic, selfish people who want to inflict cancer on my precious lungs with their second-hand smoke. So now in most states smoking has been outlawed in bars. What a relief that bars can now be enjoyed as the healthy, wholesome places they were meant to be.

What's next? Are they going to police every supermarket checkout line? *"Lady, we're replacing this whole milk with skim, because frankly, you need it." "If you'll just cooperate, we'll allow you the Brie cheese pending the results of your blood work."*

Like most mothers, I have good intentions. I've tried to instill good eating habits in my offspring. The Books say if you start them out as babies on veggies instead of fruit they won't develop a sweet tooth. Well, the bouncing baby to whom I spoon fed organic brown rice and peas (the kid had more gas than a hot-air balloon festival in Chicago) is now a second-grader clawing at the pantry in search of a plastic fruit roll-up.

Yeah, yeah, if I didn't have the fruit roll-ups in the house they wouldn't ask for them. Well, all it takes is one "playdate" (cringe) at another kid's house that DOES have them to make your kids start nagging you relentlessly.

The books also say your kids learn from you and if you "model" good eating habits, they will too. Right. I'd like to force-feed some free-range crow to that child-rearing expert. I can shove carrot sticks in my maw in front of my kids all day, but they will still whine for the Ritz Bits (the new, awesome pizza flavor).

At this point I rejoice when my kids eat broccoli and non-fat granola bars but mostly I am defeated in my quest for organic purity. I am reduced to feelings of schadenfreude when the organic kid gets Coxsackie at the town pool anyway despite his superior immune system.

Please Don't Call Child Protection Services

Heaven help you these days if you have a klutz for a kid. I had to explain his latest injury to his teacher. It was a huge goose egg on his forehead. He acquired this third eye from taking a flying leap toward a glass French door. He's the only kid in the class picture who is wearing his band-aids as proudly as the little girls are wearing their new Princess Barbie barrettes.

I always wonder what kind of tone of voice should I use to stave off potential suspicion. Laugh-it-off seasoned mom, contrite worried mom, or giggling nervously I-swear-I-don't-have-Munchausen's-by-proxy-syndrome mom.

There's an accident-prone child in every family, but lucky me, I have three. When I brought my oldest in for his first dental check-up at age two, the dentist noticed the huge scratch across his cheek and eyed me suspiciously. "Where did he get THAT?"

I was so taken aback that I'm sure I stammered something mildly self-incriminating. Naturally I thought of a better response later. Something along the lines of, say, "Well, he got it from me. You see, I gouged his cheek on purpose before I brought him in for a preventative dental check-up. Next time I'll wait until after the appointment to abuse him."

Maybe it has something to do with having boys. I think Mothers Of Only Daughters (MOODies) are slightly horrified when my rag-tag bunch shows up bruised, battered and bouncing all over the place, smashing their trucks together. THEIR darling daughters are sitting nicely making cupcakes out of Play-Doh for their tea party, or whatever it is little girls do before they turn to tormenting their peers over weight issues. Go ahead girl-moms, be smug. I may be on a first name basis with the triage nurse in the ER, but at least I get to avoid like the plague the Pepto-Pink aisle at Toys R Us.

My point is that there is a whole new level of suspicion about child abuse than there was when we were kids. Mostly this is a good thing, of course. But the fall-out is that new moms have to awkwardly apologize for every bruise, zit or bee sting. You can't win. If you don't mention it, you look guilty. If you do bring it up, you look guilty.

Much well-meaning suspicion is misdirected. Real child abuse often goes unreported while moms of toddlers everywhere are dressing their kids in leggings and parkas for a day at the beach just to avoid scrutiny.

A friend of mine was court-martialed by the kindergarten teacher and school principal. Her child was supposed to be picked up by a neighbor, but the neighbor forgot and my friend rushed over to school to get her son. But while he waited the little darling had an entire hour to talk to the school authorities about the things his mom does. Leaves him alone with his toddler sister (she was talking to a neighbor outside), dancing with naked men (she went to a Broadway show with her husband), sending her daughter to school with no breakfast (she's two and just refused to eat that morning). The poor thing is now forced to pick up her children wearing a head scarf and Jackie-O glasses.

How about the zero-tolerance policies at schools? Suspending a kindergartner for saying *bang bang* when pointing his finger? Good thing the zero-tolerance doesn't extend to adults with anger issues, like me. I mean, what's the fun of driving if you can't flip off people driving yellow Hummers?

Are we being too careful? Jeez, take a look at playgrounds now. Well-meaning, yes, but padded, plastic, lawsuit-proof and completely boring.

Playgrounds used to be a place to push your limits, get scraped up and find your place in the social pecking order. Asphalt, steel and splintered wood used to be the materials of choice. Every summer scores of kids faced Bactine, tweezers, and those tell-tale orange disinfectant stains that took weeks to fade. I never see kids with broken arms anymore. That's a good thing, right?

How are our kids going to know how far they can push their limits? We have protected them so much that perhaps they are not developing their own instincts and survival skills. Ten bucks someone will figure this out and sell us an interactive program so our kids can practice their survival skills in a safe, supervised and climate-controlled environment. Some software with questions like:

If Johnny jumps off that tree limb, will he break his leg or just sprain an ankle?

It's getting dark. Who's hiding behind that shrub? Is it the newly-released sex offender or your puppy, Dingleberry?

Only a generation ago our moms used to let us go out with our bikes and told us to come home when it got dark. How about that time when you stayed out a little too long and faced a scary ride home? You knew it was your own fault, and you alone had to make it home. But you did it, felt infinitely stronger for it, and you knew not to do it again. How will our kids learn those lessons? That's not something you can teach at Sylvan.

Mean Old Ladies

OK, what's the deal, seniors? Have you completely forgotten what it's like to raise kids? Why do you give us such withering looks when our toddler has a fit in the check out line? This never happened to you? Kids were that much different in the fifties?

Hey, give me a break. I'm sorry I planned my fun-filled shopping trip for the same time the senior citizen bus drops all of you off, but I was out of juice boxes. I just cannot be out of juice boxes. I'll lose my union card and they'll send my kids off to foster care.

Look, I try to be understanding. I mean, I'm going to be old some day if my kids don't kill me first. I try to be patient when they park their carts in the middle of the aisle. I gingerly move them aside, in a manner I hope suggests my goodness as a human being, that is, with a pleasant smile on my face. I don't want to seem like I'm in a hurry, even though I have to finish this shopping trip in fourteen minutes or I'll be late again for T-Ball practice. I want to be helpful, so I happily grab canned peaches off the top shelf for them if they ask. I patiently submit to their lectures when I grab the first orange juice I see and not the brand that's on sale.

So I'm just asking for the same respect in return! Don't give me the evil eye if my darlings brush against your cart while they jump from green linoleum square to the next green linoleum square. After all, they have to avoid the red squares. Those are the "lava."

I hope when I'm older I'll remember every last thing about how tough it is to get through a grocery store trip with three reluctant boys trailing behind me. The preschooler had to open and shut every single frozen food section door, in precise order (the pediatrician tells me OCD is normal for this age). The kindergartner was begging for an orange soda and had to go potty. The second grader was lecturing me on the food pyramid. He wanted a detailed explanation of what "price per unit" means and then started whining "but I don't GET it" after I tried to explain it.

I wound up with fruit roll-ups, library paste and a Buzz Lightyear toothbrush not because I'm worthless and weak, but because you can only say NO 2.364 times before you finally say YES, DAMMIT, I'LL BUY THE F***ING FROOT LOOPS!

It was even worse when they were babies. I remember trying to balance that bloody car seat on the shopping cart, rushing through a shopping trip, forgetting the milk, butter and eggs, only to have my odiferous heir wake up and scream in the check out line while I was leaking milk like the Johnstown dam. And then I get The Look from the old lady behind me. That tongue-clucking they all do. "You should have gotten a babysitter. In our day we didn't take kids shopping." Right.

In your day, old woman, they had pushcarts and milkmen. You didn't have to leave the house, remember? So don't mess with me. I'm sleep-deprived, my tits are ready to blow and my husband's working late again so you gotta ask yourself 'Do I feel lucky? Well, do ya, punk?'

I hope when I'm old I'll give understanding looks to the struggling young mothers. I want to be the cool old lady that all the new moms dig. I'll dispense thoughtful advice and well-timed dum-dum lollipops. And when some poor, hapless mother is desperately trying to soothe an overtired toddler in the cereal aisle, I'll lean over and whisper, "Just buy him the f***ing Froot Loops. It worked in our day."

WonderMom-ism: A Study in Acceptance and Recovery

We all know burned-out, achievement-oriented women who have left high-powered careers in order to experience the joy of staying home to raise their children. They figure if they can run things at the office efficiently, surely the challenges of running a home should be a piece of cake.

But in no time at all they are on their knees searching for the lost pacifier, smashing wayward Cheerios in the process, as the squalling toddler topples out of the high chair. Before long they would rather take a beating than play another game of *Candy-Land.* This was not as they pictured it.

Of course not. You cannot compare the working life to staying at home with children. At least in the office there is some semblance of logic and order, however strained at times. Most likely you will not have to deal with someone who insists on being nude all day. Usually your co-workers will be able to speak when they want something instead of pointing at the air, wetting themselves and screaming.

But these earnest mothers don't understand they are dealing with a completely logic-free paradigm, to quote an over-used management term. They just try harder to impose order upon the shifting sands. Consciously or not, desperately in need of a challenge, they make the decision to become the best stay-at-home moms ever.

They set impossible goals. They see themselves dancing around a sparkling home wearing MAC lipstick and Jimmy Choo's. The children's scrapbooks will be arranged chronologically in the polished bookcase, and of course there will always be organic carob-chip cookies in the oven.

Sisters, it's the fast lane to the Funny Farm, and we've all been there.

All of us stay-at-homes have fallen prey to this mentality to some degree. We compare ourselves endlessly to other mothers. This one has three kids who have won early-acceptance to Princeton. That one brings her kids to Guatemala to build houses for Habitat for Humanity. God, what's wrong with us? We can't even remember to put the wet laundry in the dryer before it starts a'stinkin'.

So we try harder. We hit the craft stores and stock up on pipe cleaners and Elmer's glue so our children can have the tools at hand to become the next Calder. We read *The Canterbury Tales* to the toddlers instead of *Stop Picking Your Nose, Elmo!* We spend hours planning and decorating the perfect nursery that our kids won't even remember.

We don't recognize that we are on the slippery slope to WonderMom-ism until it's too late. One day we find we can't stop reading Penelope Leach once we start. We begin lying about the mountain of educational computer games we purchased for our kids. We start to hide the cartons of toilet paper cores we're saving for craft projects. It's time to wake up and smell the DiaperGenie.

At this point every mother has to take a long look in the mirror. Alone. No playgroup can help you now.

Admit that you turn to putty before fear-producing books like *Incredibly Tedious Kitchen Counter-Staining Crafts You Should Be Doing With Your Kids Or Else They'll Wind Up Living In Your Basement Until They're Forty.* Accept that the notices jonesing for field trip chaperones will always be sent home in the backpacks, but you must find a way to fight the urge within you to say *yes I said yes I will Yes!*

Once you realize that you are a WonderMom wannabe you will be in recovery for the rest of your life. Take it one day at a time.

As with other obsessive, addictive diseases, you have to hit rock bottom before you can climb your way back to sobriety. Rock bottom for me was my frugal phase. I read somewhere that I could save a quarter every time I hung the wash to dry instead of using the dryer. So what if the towels dried in this manner could shred skin. I kept thinking of the quarters! That's when I knew I needed help.

Luckily I went through the twelve steps successfully. Step Three was the toughest. That's the one where I had to get store-bought valentines instead of making them with my kids. Step Six was bad too. I had to throw away every masterpiece sent home from preschool, layer by layer, until I could see my refrigerator again. And Step Nine, whew, that sucked. I had to say no to three separate Girl Scouts hawking Thin Mints. When I got to Step Twelve and let somebody else be the class parent for the year, I knew I could stick with the program even though I was a sweaty, shaking mess.

It's easy to see how WonderMom-ism develops. We see Mothering as a new career. But it's not a career. It's just living. Most of us have a lot less training for that. I'm reading right out of the recovery manual now, can you tell?

The awful thing all WonderMoms must eventually face is that kids don't necessarily need or want constant planned activity. Once they're past a certain age they just want to know you are there for speedy snack delivery or to recover their favorite Hot Wheels car from underneath the sofa where it had gone to die in peace. It got to the point where my guys would groan pitifully and shuffle into the kitchen whenever I announced a new craft project in my "I'm a Sunny Mommy" voice.

Please join me in recovery. It's a freeing feeling when you stop trying to be WonderMom. We have a great time at the meetings. We feed the kids an occasional nugget of processed food and no one gasps in disbelief. We often tell the children to stop interrupting the grown-ups and go find something else to do. If one of us says, "No, I will not read *Goodnight, Moon* again. Just go to sleep already." Cheers and huzzahs are heard.

We've stopped pretending that playing *Hi-Ho Cherry-O* is a Kodak moment. If you wanted to cry the last time you spun the empty bucket, thereby prolonging the game another 25 minutes, you're one of us. But if you thought, "great, more time to practice our number skills!" you may not be ready for the twelve steps just yet.

Recovering WonderMoms like to be alone once in awhile. We're here for you, darlings, but we just want to pee by ourselves. The door is locked because we don't want to let you into the bathroom anymore. We don't want to seize the moment to talk about why girls don't have penises but can still pee. And we sure as heck don't want a photo of that in a custom-designed scrapbook.

Beautiful People Make Better Mothers

Elizabeth Hurley lost her baby weight faster than YOU did. Look! Pamela Anderson can give birth and blow her husband at the same time! Cindy Crawford looked better pushing her baby out than you looked at your wedding! Sarah Jessica Parker walked out of the maternity ward wearing Manolo Blahniks!

Listen up, *People, Us,* paparazzi and celebrity chasers: STOP IT! Please stop showing us the whole folksy celebrities-as-parents thing. We can't stand it anymore. It's bad enough that they parade around like they are the first women to ever have given birth. But when you've got the 3am postpartum weepies, every cell of your body aches and you're trying to quiet a colicky, sadistic infant the last thing you need to hear is that Cindy Crawford was back at yoga in one week. Cindy, I've got your Downward Facing Dog right here. And she bites.

I don't want to know how wonderful their lives are! Oh look, there's Calista Flockhart with her kid and he's having a tantrum. Wow, those beautiful celebs must be just like us! Right. You know she handed the brat off to the nanny when she got home and popped a Xanax. Plus she gets to sleep with Harrison Ford, for crissake. I think I could deal with my kid's tantrum if I knew Indiana Jones was waiting for me between the sheets.

Motherhood is hard enough without comparing ourselves to celebs. Our culture is so enamored of these people that we are utterly amazed when they do something mundane. Wow! Matthew Broderick went out to eat and he was looking sleep-deprived because he's a new Dad! We're supposed to say, "Aw, ain't that sweet!" but instead we are really thinking "must be nice to get out to dinner, you lucky S.O.B. What is it, the cook's day off?"

I also love the celebs who say, "Oh, I really lead a very dull, normal life." Shut up. You know what? Normal does NOT involve having a movie premiere to go to this weekend. A personal umbrella handler and your name on a director's chair have nothing to do with dull and ordinary. Just because you pick up your own kid from school when you're not on location does not mean you're one of us.

Nobody tells us how wonderful we are when we take our kids to the park. Nobody asks us our secret when we manage to get back into our old jeans. We labor in obscurity, forever, with no hope of rescue, relief, or Dolce and Gabbana. That's what normal is.

Not only are we forced to look at how lovely and spoiled the stars are, we are also forced to listen to their parenting advice.

Madonna doesn't allow her kids to watch TV, oh scratch that, has instructed her team of nannies not to let the kids watch TV, because it's evil. Oh please. *Madonna* is preaching to us on morals? Did I miss something? What's next, the Pope's Missive on Marital Aids? Madge, get real. If you were home alone trying to get dinner going, helping with spelling homework, dealing with an explosive diaper, and trying to keep the toddler out of the poop all at the same time, you would have *Sesame Street* on the idiot box faster than you can say "Papa Don't Preach."

There is just no way they could ever have the smallest dust mote of a clue what it is like to raise children like the rest of us. Yes, all parents adore their kids and worry about them, but anybody could do it part-time, with tons of money and support, and think they are really getting down to the nitty-gritty of parenting. It's the 24/7 for 18 +years that will wear you down. They are in a completely different league so don't try to convince us otherwise by showing us pictures of a Prada-clad Angelina Jolie taking her kid to a playground.

I would love to see how fast celeb moms could get back to looking gorgeous without nannies, personal trainers, personal assistants, masseuses, spa vacations, stylists, make-up artists, home-delivered meals, money and a full-night's sleep. I'd give them one week before they would be wallowing in the shit like the rest of us.

I'm envisioning Sarah Jessica stuffing Oreos into her pie-hole while rustling through Matthew's closet for a big shirt to cover the maternity leggings she's still wearing. She's teary because her fave Blahniks won't fit since her feet have gone up a whole size since the baby. And like the rest of us, there's no money for a new pair. She hasn't been out of the 500 square-foot apartment all day and hasn't even brushed her teeth. The only aromatherapy facial she's going to be getting is when her son pees on her face during a diaper change. Try living like this for a few months. Then maybe I'll listen when you tell me how wonderful life is with a newborn.

Us magazine takes pictures of pregnant celebs and points to their "bumps." Since when are pregnant bellies called "bumps"? How cute. For the rest of us, I think a more realistic term might be "staggeringly huge stomach" or "spine-busting, kidney-rupturing mountain of future heir." Speaking from experience, I don't think it would be too amusing to follow us nobodies around when we're pregnant, taking pictures of our stomachs for a "bump watch."

At five months I was so huge that complete strangers would ask, "when are you due??" and, "oh my *God*, can I get you a cab?" As I waddled down the sidewalk people would catch sight of my stomach and their eyes would widen comically. It's disconcerting to have horrified onlookers move to the side so you can pass. At nine months, *Us* would have to run my picture as a two-page spread.

God knows we try our pathetic best to look good. We see an article about the beautiful new strappy sandals that glam moms Elle McPherson and Uma Thurman are buying. Of course, our feet have more cracks than dried-out Play-Doh but we put the kid in the bouncy seat next to the shower, and in we go to sand off the crud with all the new supplies we just got at CVS. Any seasoned mother knows the child will start to cry the minute your hair is full of suds. Hurry! Rinse off while you are envisioning your child tipping over, knocking himself out and child services coming and taking him away. The newspaper will report that while your child was in peril you were sanding your feet with a smelly pumice stone. After a few fruitless attempts at self-beautification the burqa doesn't seem like such a bad idea.

And now here's the latest *People.* Oh goody. Some gorgeous celeb is knocked up again. Doesn't she look marvelous? Listen up, Princess. Don't venture into our 'hood, the land of the great unwashed and unchic. The huddled masses yearning to breathe free. We WILL hurt you. There are a lot of seething mothers here who hope you develop a set of hemorrhoids so big that you'll have to find room for them next to your handprints on the Walk Of Fame. Shut up and have the kid already and if we hear that you had an easy labor you better watch your back on the red carpet, Missy.

The Precious Child Syndrome

I knew I was in trouble when I opened the mail. The outside of the envelope read "*Your child speaks ONLY English?*" Inside was a brochure for a French enrichment program that cost more than my first car. And my second and third, come to think of it. Here I thought I was doing okay because the kid was finally talking (I was blessed with three, count 'em, three late talkers) and now I have to worry because he can't, oh, how you say ... *parlez un fucking mot de la francaise?*

More evidence of the Precious Child Syndrome. Just read the latest crop of parenting books and listen to the buzz and it's painfully obvious that parenting is a competition. No more, "Run outside and play, kids. Mommy's having the girls over for bridge and Black Russians." Now it's all about achievement. More, better, and earlier than the kid next door.

I do not understand why so many parents feel they have to craft the perfect little genius. I'm not sure they've actually thought this through. Do they really want their kids to be able to smart-mouth them in Mandarin Chinese? Can they possibly want pasty-skinned kids who would rather make a wicked chess move than make out under the bleachers? Do they really want their kids to be the ones explaining the meaning behind off-color Latin puns?

The pressure to compete now is just inescapable. It's never too young to expose them to the best. Don't let your child get left behind while your neighbor's kid is first viola with the New York Philharmonic. What! You haven't started little Preston on skates yet! He's already three! At this rate he'll never make the traveling hockey team! Just forget it, it's too late for him already. Never mind that he's only been walking for two years. You hear it all the time. All the best players started *before they could walk.*

It's very disturbing if you happen to have a child who is not among the elite preschool prodigies. What about the kids who are late bloomers, like my gaggle of klutzes? Is it really all over for my kid when he cries on the soccer field at age four because some daddy-driven hotshot in regulation regalia stole the ball from him? Are there only atomic wedgies in his future?

When we were kids there was a whole lot less of this nonsense. Sure, there were little leagues and swim teams but it didn't seem to really get competitive until around middle school. By that age many more kids were ready for a more intense level of competition. Fewer kids got left out.

And the academics! Maybe I grew up in an intellectually-challenged locale but NO ONE I knew took an SAT prep class. It just wasn't done. We were all too busy peeling the labels off of Michelob bottles and trying to look old enough to get into the bars. Somehow we all managed to get into excellent universities and go on to lead fulfilled, productive adult lives. Well, except in my case. I was an art major.

NO ONE took piano lessons at four, or karate, or kiddie yoga for crissake. We just PLAYED. Tag, bike riding, *Mad Libs*, setting fire to green army men, that sort of thing. We used to put grasshoppers under magnifying glasses, but WE didn't have to live under them.

This trend towards overscheduling and hyper-achievement has been well documented of late, but speaking from the trenches I don't see things changing. My fourth grader, who happens to be a bright, conscientious kid, had over four hours of homework the other night. (No, he doesn't go to private school.) This is a kid who used to like learning and now sees the whole mess as an anxiety-producing hell. Great.

While this is going on we have parents, in our school district, who are saying the schools are being dumbed down and the test scores aren't high enough. They are demanding homework be sent home in Kindergarten. I don't understand what it is they are expecting. I see fourth graders learning concepts I didn't study until high school. What's the bloody rush?

I wonder what this generation will look like when it comes of age. It will be an awe-inspiring thing. They have been so groomed to achieve every milestone in life early that they're even going to have to move up the age of the mid-life crisis from forty to twenty-five. At the same time I've been reading that this generation is postponing adulthood and independence longer than any generation that has come before. Imagine, having a mid-life crisis before you've moved out of your parent's basement.

It's very difficult to stand apart from all this because there is always the nagging doubt "but what if I don't give Madison those French horn lessons?" With everyone else pushing so hard has the bar really been raised? If we step away from the insanity are we consigning our children to a lifetime of underdeveloped intellect and dead-end jobs? None of us raise our kids in a vacuum. We're at the mercy of standardized testing that is tied to real estate values and Kaplan learning centers. I just read an article that those creepy Japanese cram schools are starting to spring up here and there.

You've got to wonder what these parents are really pushing for. No matter how stellar the child turns out, he or she will still be a human being. The kid's going to screw up somewhere, sometime. How will these parents handle it when Justin decides he just can't be a piano prodigy at Julliard, a Nobel Prize-winning poet and a Heisman Trophy winner all at the same time?

Some say that kids that are pushed too hard now will rebel later and suffer from burn-out. All of us slacker moms who have stepped off enrichment merry-go-round certainly hope so. We will be vindicated at last. Horrified Achiev-o parents everywhere will be shocked when their finely honed geniuses want to kick up their heels a bit. *"Oh my God! Oliver's having sex with his girlfriend and smoking pot! Where did we go wrong?"* Poor Oliver's just doing what Mom and Dad did back in the seventies in the high school parking lot, with Pink Floyd blasting from the Duster's eight-track. *We don't need no education!* You can remember that, right, Mom and Dad? That was fun, wasn't it? As for you, Oliver, you're going to be just fine. Go for it, kid, and roll me a fattie.

"THE ENVELOPE, PLEASE"

It's Time for the Mommy Awards. Sit Still, And Keep Your Hands To Yourself.

I'm utterly ashamed of myself because I watched the entire Academy Awards from start to finish. I can't believe I wasted more than three hours of my life watching a bunch of spoiled celebrities congratulate themselves. It got me thinking, though. Why has the entertainment industry cornered the market on self-aggrandizement? Why not the world's most demanding occupation?

It's time for Awards for Outstanding Achievement in Motherhood. And not some Hallmark-sponsored nonsense about awarding the best Play-Doh maker. No, it's time to award the REAL achievements of motherhood, like coming up with the best lie about your past drug use or managing to have sex in seven minutes while your kids are downstairs watching *The Fairly Odd Parents.*

What a festive night this could be! The first step would be coming up with the name of the award show. You need some sort of catchy acronym like the BASFLO awards (Bring A Sweater For Later On) or the IOOPs (I'm Only One Person!). The trophy itself should be a real symbol of motherhood, like a bronzed wooden spoon or a prescription for Paxil reproduced in platinum. Or maybe it could be a statue of a pack mule: welcome to the ASS awards ... Awed, Stunned and Sleepy.

It can start with Oscar-like buzz months ahead of the show. Who will be nominated? Everybody has an opinion. *"Lillian Facetwitch definitely deserves it. I saw her smiling even though her mother-in-law was visiting for a whole week! Now that's acting!"*

"Maybe it will be Olivia Brownbag when she said she would be happy to chaperone the lunch period at school. Did you see her blinking back the tears? Those were real tears, too! I was very moved by her performance."

Finally the nominees are announced. The lucky ones who got the nod are pursued everywhere. They are photographed furtively returning library books (three weeks late!) or standing in line at the DMV, even though they try their best to wear dark glasses and go incognito. Perhaps an angry husband might pull a Sean Penn and bust up some paparazzi while the tearful mommy pulls the minivan into the garage.

Then come the rounds of talk show interviews. Katie Couric would try to wrangle the moms' secrets out. *"How did you do it? We really believed you were interested in hearing that same Knock-Knock joke for the twenty-third time! How do you possibly prepare for such a performance?" "You can tell me, any projects coming up? I mean after the bake sale, of course."* Annie Leibowitz would photograph the Power Moms for *Vanity Fair*. Posed, lit and retouched so well you wouldn't notice the snot-decorated shoulders and the tell-tale pink amoxicillin stains. On awards night the whole country tunes in to the Barbara Walters Fuzzy Camera Lens Weep-Fest.

Finally, the big night arrives. I would like to see what that red carpet parade would look like. Mothers in their very best old bridesmaids dresses (see, you really CAN wear it again), moth-eaten Gunne Sax prom gowns and altered maternity dresses. Those remoras Melissa and Joan Rivers would be there, making their catty comments and conducting depth-challenged interviews.

"Who are you wearing?"

"Huh? Oh, it's Sears Lemon Frog shop circa 1975."

"OOOOH, VINTAGE! And that looks like a genuine Goody hair scrunchie. I just love her eclectic attitude towards style, don't you, Melissa?"

Some lucky moms might snag some borrowed jewels, not from Harry Winston but from the neighbor whose husband knows someone in the diamond district. Those heinous Mother's Day birthstone necklaces would be very happening. Naturally the tried and true macaroni and lanyard necklaces would be the must-have item of the evening, sparking scores of campy knock-offs that would appear in Target the following week.

There would be mucho buzz about the PC Statement O' The Year pin. *"Do you think she's going to wear her Cotton Ball ribbon, signifying her anti-disposable diaper bias? Or maybe the Cracked Nipple pin, honoring the La Leche league?"*

Ladies and gentlemen, please take your seats. The nebbish-y host walks out and does a bit about his own mother and therapy sessions that are a little too personal but everybody laughs politely and claps anyway. Mothers have a lot of practice doing that on any given day so it feels perfectly normal for them. Then comes the lush, sweeping montage of winning mommies of the past, like Joan Crawford and the oldest woman to give birth from the Guinness Book of World Records.

Finally it's time to announce the awards. I envision the categories breaking down something like this:

The **HELL JUST ADDED ANOTHER CIRCLE Award** is for the most believable feigned fascination.

The nominees are:

1. Mindy Chickencross for her frozen smile in "The LONGEST

JOKE EVER TOLD."

2. Susie Droolcup for sitting through a Yu-Gi-Oh marathon in "THE GOOD PART'S COMING UP."
3. Wendy Jockitch for watching her son shoot baskets in "WATCH, I PROMISE I'LL MAKE IT THIS TIME."
4. Annie Kittensmittens for reading *Goodnight Moon* thirty-seven times in "THE LITTLE OLD LADY WHISPERING HUSH."
5. Sarah Heiney for clocking 472 hours of watching her kid sit on the pot in "SHOW ME WHAT A BIG GIRL YOU ARE!"

The **SERENITY NOW! Award** is for outstanding patience during a road trip. The nominees are:

1. I.M. Desperate for successfully distracting her fighting children in "LOOK! AN ALASKA LICENSE PLATE!"
2. Amy Efficient for mastering the speedy, side-of-the-highway pit stop in "WHIP IT OUT HERE, BOYS."
3. Lydia Strongspine for her steely determination not to stop at South of the Border in "PASSING PEDRO."
4. A.L. Tryanything for her inventive approach to backseat games in "LET'S COUNT THE WAFFLE HUTS."
5. Emily Sedated for reviving the old standby in "WHO CAN BE QUIET THE LONGEST?"

The **"WHEELS ON THE BUS" Award** is for the Kid Song most likely to eat its way into your brain, take root and hang on like a binging leech. I don't even want to mention the nominees because you'll never forgive me. You'll be forever singing *"Thomas The Tank Engine Rolling Along...Thomas We Love Youuuuuu!"* Oops, sorry! Well, it's permanently stuck in my head and why should I have all the fun?

The **"DEPENDS"** award is for the scariest scene in a horror movie.

The nominees are:

1. Amy Hemorrhoids for sitting next to the kid with tons of nasty ear wax on the noxious school bus in "CHAPERONE."
2. Sadie Noisemaker for accidentally feeding cake to the kid with gluten allergies in "BIRTHDAY PARTY OF THE DAMNED."
3. Ova Menses for suddenly realizing it's Day Forty Two in "OH GOD, I CAN'T BE PREGNANT, CAN I?"
4. Lola Couchcushion for paying $22.00 at the video store for a *Dora the Explorer* video in "LATE FEES."
5. Janie Happymeal for the nightmarish search for the cheapo plastic toy her hysterical child misplaced in "HELL TO PAY."

The **SYLVIA PLATH Award** is for supreme martyrdom.

The nominees are:

1. Patty Longsuffering for taking an enriching cross-country driving vacation in a compact car with three sons fighting the entire way and never once resorting to the use of GameBoys, Nintendo or a rigged-up VCR in "ONE FLEW OVER THE CUCKOO'S NEST."
2. Ayun D. Desitin for using cloth diapers until little Whizzie was toilet trained, and not cheating once, not even on that road trip to Boise in "MY BEAUTIFUL LAUNDRETTE."
3. Soya Hippiedippie for refusing to feed her children anything but organic, and never caving once even though her kids completely lost their shit in the supermarket begging for Scooby-Doo Big Berry Blast Fruit Roll-Ups in "THE GRAPES OF WRATH."
4. N. Gorge Letdown for nursing her twins Romulus and Remus

their entire first year and not using any bottles, not even when she eventually went mad, wore her nursing bra as a hat and was committed in "WHATEVER HAPPENED TO BABY JANE?"

The **MEA MAXIMA CULPA Award** for outstanding achievement in bad mothering.

The nominees are:

1. Carie Sealent for refusing to floss her kids teeth, even after a receiving a stern talking-to from the pediatric dentist (who really needs to get out more) in "I HAVE BETTER THINGS TO DO."
2. Kathy Givehertheslip for hiding from the mom to whom she owes playdates in "BEHIND THE VELVEETA DISPLAY."
3. Ivana Noclutter for trashing all the crappy kid-art masterpieces when her children weren't looking in "AIN'T NO REFRIGERATOR BIG ENOUGH."
4. Mindy Fed-Up for feeding her kids cereal for dinner again in "TEN VITAMINS AND IRON."
5. I. Giveup for burning all of her child rearing books in "WHO'S AFRAID OF PENELOPE LEACH?"

The **BABY BOP Award** goes to the kiddie show character you just want to fucking strangle. The nominees are:

1. All of those bastards from *The Wiggles.*
2. That maniacally-smiling mechanic from "*Jay-Jay the Jet Plane.*"
3. The dog Blue, because of that weedling bark/whine sound it makes. CHRIST, MAKE IT STOP!
4. Raffi's endangered baby beluga.
5. That hideous two-headed dragon in "Dragon Tales." What the hell IS that?

The nominees for most hilarious, outrageous, unbelievable comedy:
1. Sleep When The Baby Sleeps
2. Finding Time For Yourself
3. The Family Bed
4. At Six Weeks Postpartum You Can Resume Your Regular Sex Life
5. They Grow Up So Fast

The nominees for most tragic, tear-jerking drama:
1. Still In Maternity Jeans
2. If The Shower's On At 2am It Must Be Croup
3. *Next Rest Stop 45 Miles*
4. Sent Back To The Start Of Chutes And Ladders
5. The Pizza Delivery Guy Just Quit

There would be a version of the Thalberg award for lifetime achievement. This year's winner is Betty Fairplay who managed to pour the last bit of remaining calcium-enriched orange juice into three cups in EXACTLY EVEN AMOUNTS! Past winners include the woman whose annual pagan bonfire of Little Tykes coupes became a neighborhood tradition and Whinny, the Wonder Mom, who managed to nail "Magenta" with some rotten tomatoes during the "Blues Clues Live" show before she was finally arrested.

I don't think you would see any phony "Oh I'm so happy she won" fake smiles and applause from the losers. Just honest-to-goodness pouting, glowering and jealousy. *"I'll fix your wagon at the school fair, bitch." "You can forget about that playdate next week, Miss Statue-Winner."*

The winner gets up, trips on the stairs (natch) and starts her speech. *"Oh I can't believe I won! I'm absolutely shocked! Why, here's my pre-written speech and list of people to thank. I have to thank the stoner babysitter at the gym, the Rhinovirus Nursery School, the makers of Flintstones vitamins, Mylicon drops and Percoset. To all my fellow nominees: I'm so honored to be in your company. This belongs to all of you!"* Then she heads the wrong way till the presenter turns her around and leads her into the press room, where she stands like a deer in the headlights facing flashes and microphones. "How do you feel after winning?" "Actually, I can't feel a thing. This show's so long my ass fell asleep two hours ago and my tits are so engorged I busted my darts."

Sitting through a boring four-hour awards show might sound like torture to anyone else, but most mothers will do anything for an evening away from the housenadkids. (I even offered to have my tubes tied so I could have a night on my own in the hospital.) To tired moms it would be a night blissfully free of Hi-Ho Cherry-O, clinging bodies and dirty butts. It sure would be nice to get some recognition for a change. And maybe even a stylist. God knows we could use one.

Coming Soon: Horny Suburban Moms Tell All!

I don't buy into that crap they put in the chick/mommy mags about the things you should do when "your man" is away. Like give yourself a manicure. Condition your hair with olive oil while wearing cucumber slices over your eyes (has anyone ever really done that?). Take a bubble bath, give yourself a bikini wax and watch *Steel Magnolias.* Yawn. Bore me fucking later.

My recipe for a fun night at home, after the kids are asleep, and "my man" is away, goes a little something like this:

1. Get yo'self a big Flintstones jelly glass or three of Chardonnay out of the box in the fridge and a DVD of *Last of the Mohicans.* It's just you, Daniel Day-Lewis and your filthy imagination.
2. Check out that scene where she says "What are you looking at, sir?" and he says "Why, I'm looking at you, miss." Holy *shit.*
3. Electronic enhancement is optional.
4. Repeat as needed.

Go ahead and laugh but don't knock it till you've tried it. It definitely beats bleaching your mustache as a way to pass the time. Um, not that I would know. But I say it's good to use your imagination to get through the mind-numbing motherhood experience. Make it a Blockbuster night, sister. Choose your poison. For me, it's Hawkeye and his, er, long rifle.

I love that line I read somewhere once: women reach their sexual peak about the time men are discovering they have a favorite chair. My girlfriends and I are about as pathetic at forty as our husbands were in middle school. Frustrated, horny, bad skin. There are days when the quiet routine of married life can seem like falling on a fire ant hill in slow motion, and we're suddenly itchy for ... what was it again?

Is this the sexual peak we've been waiting for or did we miss it while waiting in the deli line? We've all been told it's supposed to hit around this age. And if this is the real thing, what do we do now? Talk about being all dressed up and having no place to go!

So here we are, forty and boy-crazy. We sit around like we're back in school and scan celebrity rags like they were yearbooks. We talk about George Clooney like he was the sexy square-jawed quarterback who didn't know we were alive. And what we would do to him ... .well, you get the idea.

Even before the drinks are served the girls' night out conversation invariably defaults to sex. How often you and your husband do it, if at all, any unusual proclivities, anatomical descriptions that would make a urologist gag. Who's got a vibrator, who watches porn on the sly, the weirdest places you've done it, old boyfriend penis statistics, you know, the usual.

I have a friend who is a very soft-spoken, happily married mother of three. One night after many pints her gentle demeanor was pulled off faster than, well, Clooney's basketball shorts would be if he got too close to us. In its stead was the horny biker chick that's been living inside her Talbot's clothes all this time. She eyed the hotties at the pub and slurred in a hard livin' Lucinda Williams-like voice: "I don't know what's wrong with me lately. I see a cute guy and I think ... I want to get you in the mud and fuck you like a dog."

It's hardly news that women can talk dirty when they're together. However, it might be news that MOTHERS can talk dirtier than anyone could ever imagine. For some reason it disturbs people that mothers get horny. Society's picture of motherhood doesn't have a place for those of us who are furtively Googling our old boyfriends while the kids watch *Avatar.*

Single women get to be horny and sleep around. Us mothers have to resort to talking about Barishnikov's ass in those tights.

I think the memory of what it's really like to date gets fuzzy, like the memories of childbirth. We fantasize about it being glam and exciting like *Sex and the City*. But really, dating IS like childbirth. The Mystery Date Bum shows up at your door to take you out, or the OB is yelling '*push*'. Either way you're thinking: "I forgot how much this sucks and it's too late to back out now."

So we're kind of stuck. A little well-lit, nicely edited Hollywood fantasy is about as wild as we're able to get. We can make the most of it, though. Just for the record, my um, most *inspiring* scenes include but are in no way limited to: Liam Neeson emerging nude from the lake in *Rob Roy*, anything Alan Rickman says or does in *Sense and Sensibility*, when Jude Law and what's-her-name make love in *Cold Mountain*, and of course Daniel Day-Lewis' reunion scene with what's-her-face in *The Unbearable Lightness of Being*. Sigh. Any of you guys can call me anytime. I have a thing for guys from England or Ireland. Maybe it's the accent. Or the teeth. Or maybe it's the fact that they are blissfully ignorant of NASCAR trivia, I don't know. But they make me swoon.

For one of my friends, Russell Crowe in *Gladiator* does it. (Oh yeah, she's *entertained* alright.) For another, it's Johnny Depp in *Chocolat*. One melts at the sight of Mel Gibson's arms in *Braveheart*. These wonderful men never have morning breath, leave floaters in the toilet or scratch their nuts when they awaken.

They don't moon you when they bend over to spit out the toothpaste and give a whole new meaning to the term "aromatherapy."

They never act like children in traffic, or make you watch them flip TV channels all night until you begin to have grand mal seizures. They are everything a husband isn't. You catch yourself when the movie scene ends sitting there, head turned to the side, mouth agape, unblinking. Maybe there's a little drool happening. You give yourself a shake, return to your previously scheduled life and think ... *shit. Time to make the donuts.*

You'd think it would be paradise being married to these studmuffins, but I'll wager even the wives of Liam, Russell, Daniel and Mel need a break now and then. (Especially Mrs. Mel! They have like, what, twenty three kids?) Living with pure raw masculine perfection 24/7 would tend wear a girl out. Imagine scores of women throwing themselves at your husband. You would have to be sexy and fascinating all the time! Think about it. No asking your husband if you have any boogers before you go into the party. No letting your belly hang out while you watch *Iron Chef.*

Maybe the Wives Of Hotties ® fantasize about guys who have lower standards, so they could eat some garlic shrimp every once in a while. I'll bet Mrs. Mel is totally hot for her deli man and makes up any excuse to run out for extra tongue. Ah-hem. And perhaps the predictable normalcy of her CPA makes Mrs. Liam get all giggly when he discusses rising interest rates, if you know what I mean.

I don't remember being so ... imaginative ... in my private life before. I guess it just wasn't necessary. Real life was pretty thrilling on its own. Now, well, thrilling is when my fave brand of juice boxes goes on sale. So why not just spice up the marriage? Oh man, that's just too depressing to contemplate. It's always the same advice.

Try some exotic lingerie.

There is just no way I'm putting on a French maid's outfit. We would just look at each other, realize that it's totally dumb, make popcorn and forget the whole thing.

Light some candles. It helps set a romantic mood.

Hell, we could fire up the entire Yankee Candle factory and it would still just be us.

Put on some sexy music.

Sexual Healing would make us roll our eyes. *Lay Lady Lay* is okay, I guess, if one happens to have a big brass bed. We don't. *Bolero* is too contrived. And *Baby Got Back* is completely out of the question.

Go on a date together.

Head down to the Indian place. Stare at each other over the sag paneer and talk about the kids all night.

Does any of this ever work? Of course not. It's just the filler they put in the women's mags along with futile tips on buying the most flattering swimsuit. Everybody knows it's hopeless. I think some more realistic article titles might be: "*How lowering my expectations saved my marriage*" and "*Why have sex when he's happy with a handjob?.*"

So that's it. Not a lot of romance on the horizon. It's clear what my only option is. My husband's traveling this week. Tonight I'm not a mom wearing Costco jeans and a bread bag twist-tie for a scrunchie. Oh no. Tonight I've become my alter ego, Madeleine Stowe. My bodice is busted and Daniel is running towards me to save me from the Hurons. Kids, get your own glass of water. Mommy's busy.

"Zen Mama"

You know that unsettling feeling you get when you look at your husband of thirteen years and you suddenly think, who the hell are you and why are you in my bed?

This is the man who held your knees behind your head throughout three labors, fed you ice chips and kindly lied when you asked him afterwards if you pooped during the pushing stage. The man who knows to steer clear of your evil twin in the morning. But for just a second, he's a complete stranger.

Or how about the time you find yourself applauding the huge log in the potty chair to which your kid has finally gave birth. You suddenly stop and cock your head like a dog when he hears a funny noise. The fog clears and you get a sparkling clear picture of where your life is at for that particular second.

You try to hold onto that moment of clarity, thinking maybe it will tell you something enlightening and useful. Maybe it's a road map pointing the way out of the maze of cloaking coping skills you've built up over a lifetime. A new consciousness that will shake off the old torpor. But you can't hold onto it, no matter how hard you try. It slips out of your grasp. Maybe that's a good thing. Perhaps it's impossible to function on a day-to-day level with that much awareness of your situation.

Oh, well. As I always say, denial is your friend. We all have our ways of masking reality.

"We just live in the burbs temporarily. When the kids are in college we'll sell the place and get a studio in the city. Only fifteen years to go."

"Yeah, I could still pull off a bikini if I lost a few pounds."

"Heck, with a little Botox I could get Ashton Kutcher too!"

"I may never drive off-road in this SUV, but at least I know I could if I wanted to."

But maybe those little flashes of clarity we all get from time to time are gifts. Instead of robotically going through our days living in denial, we get to see ourselves clearly for a moment. And if you do this, there is just no way you can look at yourself without laughing. That's why it's a gift. We can learn not to take ourselves so seriously.

Do any of these flashes of zen clarity seem familiar to you?

"Here I am, forty years old and crying tears of frustration because I can't assemble a K'nex roller coaster."

"I am fishing chunks of kid vomit out of my shower drain."

"I just sniffed my toddler's ass in public."

"I am trying to squeeze my body into a kindergarten chair at Back to School Night, in a room with thirty other adults doing the same thing."

"I am on my hands and knees looking for a Hot Wheels car under the stove, and a dried pea dropped at last night's dinner has just pierced my kneecap."

"I am completely losing my shit and any ounce of dignity I ever possessed over the fact that my kid left his spelling notebook at school, and we have to go back to retrieve it."

"I just had to tell my child to stop licking the windows on the train."

"I'm overturning sofa cushions looking for the toy plane my kid wants to put on his Amelia Earhart windsock project."

"I'm having a conversation with another adult at McDonalds who happens to be wearing a yellow and red clown suit."

"I'm getting dressed on my knees behind the bed because my son just barged into my bedroom to ask if he can have some Skittles."

"I just went to the supermarket for two items only: Huggies and Rolling Rock."

Hmm. On second thought, these flashes of clarity are not leading me to any great place. I see no higher knowledge to be gained. Better to lead a life unexamined. Son, bring me up a Rolling Rock from the basement fridge, wouldja?

Between Menarche And Matriarch: Fashion's Death Zone

I don't remember what made me search through my closet so frantically on that dark day. Maybe it was receiving that invite to a black-tie wake. Maybe I was a little unstable because I was still worried about Jennifer Aniston's adjustment to life after Brad. All I remember is the bed was piled a foot high with clothes and I was still standing there nude, flabby and teary.

This happens to me every so often. Sometimes I want to try a new look. I feel the need to show up at the town pool in something other than my husband's pit-stained tee shirt.

Maybe it's my mid-life crisis. I'm milking it for all it's worth. I'm panicked because this is my last chance to look passably hot, as long as I'm not seen in direct sunlight. I think it might be time to, gulp, go shopping again.

With my limited means and my lack of a need for couture, I figured the Gap would have something for me. I mean, I'm not completely geriatric yet. But when I walked through the hallowed doors I realized immediately that I am what trend watchers call "a Late Adapter."

I don't think there was a top in the entire place that covered the midriff. Wasn't hiding one's stomach the whole point of clothes? How long is this "lowrider-jeans-with-exposed-inner-tube-of-fat" look going to stick around, anyway?

I was seeing way more teenage butt crack and thong than I ever wanted to see. Criminy, I remember the days when "I see London I see France I see someone's underpants!" sung at you meant agonizing social death.

Then I noticed the tube tops. The Edsel of the fashion world. I thought they mercifully died off back around the time that guy from *Saturday Night Fever* jumped off the Verrazano Narrows Bridge. Good Lord, me in a tube top! Do they have any with underwire and hydraulics built in?

I found some employees who graciously took time off from their grueling "OMIGAWD" practice to help me out. I managed to find some jeans and when I paid for them they threw in a promotional Madonna/Missy Elliot CD. As if either of them actually shop in the Gap.

Women who are around my age remember all these funky fashions from the first time around. We could pull it off when we were seventeen and had stomachs so flat you could balance a bottle of Michelob on them.

The things I could get away with! I could go braless without the National Guard being called in and mothers covering the eyes of their children. I could wear cut-off shorts, cowboy boots and a cowboy hat to an Outlaws concert and no one even pointed and laughed.

Feeling depressed and decrepit, and not wanting to admit I could not name even one Missy Elliot song, I shuffled home.

It doesn't help that us stay-at-home moms tend to let ourselves go. We think 'Oh, who's going to see me, anyway? Another Cinnabon? Why the hell not?'

It starts with the baseball cap over dirty hair. The next thing you know you're dropping off your kid at school with stubbly legs poking out of safety-pinned shorts (the button popped), wearing a tee-shirt decorated with toothpaste dribbles. It's makeover time.

But TV makeovers are completely impractical. The outfits they put on these agreeable souls are great if your work involves holding up the number cards between fight rounds, but I'm not putting on anything that requires whale-bone foundation garments just to volunteer in the school library.

I keep holding on to the fantasy that I'm going to collect a really chic, modular wardrobe I can wear everyday. I'll bring home the nifty blouse and the funky bag, but by the next week I'm back to looking like a panhandler because I tend to buy things that go with nothing I already have.

Every time I flip through my closet I wonder what could possibly have been going through my mind that would make my buy sequined purple suede stilettos. When it comes to making fashion decisions, I'm as flummoxed as Keanu Reeves taking his GMATs.

Here's what would truly simplify my life: Gar-animals for grownups. Do you remember that children's clothes concept from the seventies? Colorblind mothers would match a lion bottom with a lion top *et voila*! Instant Little Lord Fauntleroy! I need that now. But the matching tag symbols would have to change for adult clothes, I guess. F'rinstance, don't match a Dirty Martini to a Cosmopolitan or a Diaphragm to a Depo-Provera or you'll be featured in the Fashion Police section of *Us* magazine.

I suppose I'm just too lazy to spend that much time thinking about my clothes. I'm not willing to put in the research. When I pick up a fashion mag to see what the New Black will be I suddenly develop adult ADD. There's just too much to focus on and I wind up skipping around from page to page like an Evelyn Wood graduate on crank.

I don't have much of an eye for the cheap knockoff either. I'm not one of those people who can grab the raspberry beret and the vintage jacket and pull off A Look. I would appear about as spontaneous and natural as Dick Cheney in a tie-dyed shirt.

Still searching, I passed by the shops catering to Juniors featuring naughty tee-shirts. I can just see me at a little league game with SLUT spelled out in rhinestones across my boobs. (In my day everybody knew who the sluts were; you didn't have to advertise). (*Oh my God*, I've started saying 'in my day').

Am I to be confined to the LL Bean catalog and Sears for the rest of my life? Or dare I say it, Chadwick's? Are capris as daring as I can get now? Woooo.

So what is everyone else wearing? At school pick-up time we all check each other out, but in a very non-incriminating way. We're just desperate for ideas. Complimenting shoes always works.

"Cute slides."

"Thanks. Only $14.99 at Target."

"Really? I have to get over there."

At first glance we all wear the jeans/t-shirt uniform or some version thereof, but you have to look closer to pick up some subtleties. Sometimes these tiny differences are very revealing. For example:

Professionally done highlights: *Husband is in banking*

Home dye-job: *Husband is in the art*

Tight tee-shirt: *Showing off new boob job*

Baggy tee-shirt: *Scarfed too many munchkins at the class party*

Ponytail: *Dirty hair*

Smelly gym clothes: *Has two hours to herself in the mornings now that the baby's in preschool*

New, shiny gym clothes: *Either just joined the gym because she found out husband is cheating or it's January 2nd.*

Leggings: *New mother*

Easy-Fit jeans: *Four months pregnant*

Lipstick: *Has a parent-teacher conference*

Perfect makeup: *Has full-time help*

Jeans in August: *Spider veins*

Toe Ring: *Aging hippie chick*

Headband: *Aging Kappa*

Big smile: *First day of sleepaway camp*

New earrings: *Husband's office holiday party*

Manicure: *Bunco player*

Pedicure: *Has a podiatrist appointment*

Waxed legs and bikini area: *Is going to be induced that evening*

That was fun. But I still don't have anything to wear. Oh, the hell with it. I'll throw on my new rhinestone SLUT tee-shirt and low-rider jeans and let it all hang out. Seeing as that's the look, I'll probably be less conspicuous that way. Anything is better than L.L.Bean duck boots.

Dear your name here, Happy Holidays!

Have you ever tried to write a family newsletter at holiday time? Did you look back on the year and the only positive thing you could say about it is that you got through it?

Never fear! This Christmas/Hanukkah/Kwaanza use this helpful guide. You too can carpet-bomb the western world with an obnoxious form letter of your own, even though your family is a sorry bunch of dysfunctional losers. Feel free to refer to yourself in the third person. This is guaranteed to further annoy your nearest and dearest. Here goes:

Circle One:
A. Season's Greetings!
B. To all our blessed friends and family members, far and near!
C. Ho Ho Ho to all our vaguely-remembered former neighbors!

Circle One:
A. Can you believe that it's "holiday time" already! How "time flies"!
B. Another year has passed and we have been blessed by health and happiness.
C. Another year shot to hell.

Circle One:
A. I'm writing to you all as the "matriarch" of the "wacky and wild" Henderson bunch to bring you "up to speed!"
B. I sit with pen in hand to update you on the gifts that have been bestowed upon our family.
C. I'm writing this because it's better than watching the freakin' Grinch for the fourth time today.

Circle One:

A. To start with, yours truly is "up to her eyeballs" with her new Mary Kay business!

B. I was in charge of the bric-a-brac section of the church's rummage sale. We earned $22.75 and will donate the entire sum to the Church's legal defense fund.

C. I've started a Scrapbooking business and now my friends shun me.

Circle One:

A. Not that we need the money, mind you, with my Ted earning "VP" status this year!

B. Fred's star continues to rise at Faceless, Automaton and Howe. His new title is Vice President, Company Line Division.

C. Ned continues to crush his own dreams and ambitions in return for money to live on.

Circle One:

A. Our loveable children are just a "bundle of energy," and they sure keep me "hopping"!

B. Our immaculately-conceived children are growing by leaps and bounds, and we are in complete denial in regards to their budding sexuality.

C. Our children are still breathing, last time I checked.

Circle One:

A. Can you believe Ted junior is already 10! (oooh-I feel old!!!) He's first in the state in reading, math and general adorable freckleface-ness, routinely pitches "perfect games" in little league, is the "world's youngest" eagle scout, and loves to "tease" his little sister! Oh well, "boys will be boys"!

B. Fred junior is 10, has just received ultra early admission to Harvard, and is on the fast track for beatification.
C. Ned junior's therapist says he's making progress.

Circle One:
A. Little Madison is 8 (oooh, I feel old!!) and was a Donald Trump Honorable Mention Finalist in our county's L'il Miss Future Trophy Wife pageant! You should see "Maddy" in her costume! You would just "eat her up"!
B. Our Lexington continues to amaze us with her gymnastic talent. This year Lexi won most improved in vaulting. She loves dollhouses, horses, and donating blood at the semi-annual Red Cross Blood Drive.
C. Bowery collects gum wrappers and likes TV.

Circle One:
A. The baby is now 6 (oooh-I feel old!) and has already skipped a grade! I suppose "brilliance" just runs in the family—ha!
B. Our baby shone during his solo of the "Ave Maria" the Vienna Boys Choir.
C. Thank goodness the baby is finally out of those goddamned Pull-Ups. I thought I'd never get the smell out of the house.

Circle One:
A. The Christmas decorations are finally done, thanks to "Martha Stewart"! This year's theme is "Fruitcake Elves"!
B. The outdoor decorations took some time to get together this year, as the all-weather nativity scene is beginning to show its age. We were able to squeak out another year by leaning the magi up against the sheep.
C. Luckily we never got around to taking down the lights from

last year. All we had to do was dig the extension cord plug out of the mud behind the garbage cans.

Circle One:

A. This year we had a "fun-filled" vacation in Orlando! Epcot was just like being in "Europe" (without all the B.O. and unusual food—ha!!!!)
B. Our vacation took us to lovely Branson, Missouri, with the highlight being the Marie Osmond concert.
C. We left the kids with Mom and took the bus to Vegas. Ned walked away from the craps table with a cool fifty bucks.

Circle One:

A. Now for the sad news (Boo-Hoo): Grandpa Henderson has finally left us! He said he would make it until Willard said his name on the *Today* show, and goshdarnit, he was right! He died doing what he loved: whittling!
B. With sorrow we report the passing of Grandfather Farquehar. His memorial service at the National Cathedral was attended by hundreds who remembered his life as one full of God's blessings.
C. Not surprisingly, Grandpa finally kicked. He had been gone a few day when we found him, his hand still clasping the remote and the TV still tuned to the *Weather Channel.*

Circle One:

A. We've just been "up to our ears" with "household projects"! We were chosen as a *This Old House* project and we're getting $250,000 worth of renovations ... free! You know, Steve and Norm are REALLY nice guys!
B. We sold our house and donated the money to Habitat for Humanity. We thought it would be a growth experience for the kids.

C. We finally got around to cleaning out the garage.

Circle One:

A. Well. must dash! I'd better get back to wrapping all those presents!!!

B. I'm due at choir practice so, alas, I must bid you adieu.

C. I'd better run. I think the Christmas tree is on fire.

Circle One:

A. We can't wait to receive your card! Does *your child's name here* still have that adorable "harelip?!!!"

B. Please send some photos of your little angels.

C. Last warning…send us a card this year or you're cut off.

Circle One:

A. From all of us Hendersons ... have a "happy"!!!!

B. From our family to yours: may the blessings of the season be upon you.

C. Here's hoping a little eggnog will help you survive this cursed season.

Circle One:

A. P.S. Don't forget to put those cookies out for "you-know-who"!!! Maybe I should get him some Snackwell's—ha!

B. P.S. Don't forget that Jesus is the reason for the season.

C. P.S. Don't forget to save your receipts.

The Screaming Trees, or, A Day's Worth of School Flyers

Canned Food Drive! Let us share our bounty with the huddled masses and teeming refuse in the next town over. Please, no dented, expired cans of three-bean salad…be generous! This is not an opportunity to clean out your pantry. Cardboard boxes will be set up in the school entrance.

Join the Cub Scouts! Our homophobic, paramilitary organization has been building character for generations. Local dens now forming. Information session in the auditorium tonight. Topic: How building and racing wooden cars will bring you closer to your alienated son. Call for meeting time, which will likely be too early for fathers to attend as they will still be at work, thereby forcing their wives to take on one more child-centered activity.

We Need Homemade Goodies For The Bake Sale! No store-bought cookies please. Slice and bake is marginally acceptable. Please label all ingredients for our families afflicted with allergic children. Proceeds will benefit the PTA, but you'll never find out exactly how.

Permission Slip! Please sign and return so your child can attend the class trip to the L'il Acorns Children's Museum. We need drivers! Please indicate number of seatbelts in your car and whether or not you take any anxiety-reducing drugs on a daily basis. Charge for the trip is two dollars. No child shall be excluded due to hardship. Check this box if you don't have the two dollars and the fee will be covered by the PTA, however, they will confiscate your child's $100.00 sneakers and sell them at the rummage sale next spring as this is seen as only fair. Please sign here: Parent/guardian/distant relative/caregiver/au pair/babysitter/nanny/foster parent/enabler.

Local Jazz Concert! Enjoy the musical stylings of the Kool Katz, a hastily-thrown-together group of local musicians and expose your children to the tedium of live jazz. You know it's good for them. Concerts at inconvenient times throughout the day on Saturday at the Bean Experience! Coffeebar/Ersatz Art Gallery.

Resistance is Futile! Here are the Fall activities the recreation department is offering. Signing up for less than three ensures that community college is in your child's future. Archery (insurance waiver must be signed), Bowling (using gutter guards so no child ever experiences and learns to handle disappointment), Karate (non-refundable uniform purchase required), Formless "Creative Movement" taught by the professionals of Two Left Feat Dance Studio (child must be old enough to walk), Talented Tots Mommy and Me Clappy-Hands Feel-Good Sing-Along (bring a carpet square and join the fun with Miss Molly and her Gee-tar), Soccer Skills Clinic (in case you didn't get enough soccer the last ten months of the year), Hip-Hop and Break Dancing (no bling allowed as it scrapes the gym floor). Sign up at the rec center in person only, during ever-changing times that are totally inconvenient for working parents.

Art Enrichment! A studio intensive taught by local artists that sounds really good but will only produce decorated milk carton planters for you to wonder what to do with months from now, and items involving glitter that will fall apart upon entry to your home. Hurry and sign up today! Openings are limited, for some reason.

Pre-School Open House Night! Come and see all the local preschools give presentations, meet the directors, discuss the curriculums. Learn what all the preschools offer so you can make the right decision for your child. You'll find that they're all the same and you'll just wind up sending your child to the school that offers the extended hours option. Time: 8-10 pm in the cafeteria. Don't bother if this is your second or third child.

Swim Lessons! Nothing like changing into a swimming suit in a freezing locker room in winter, then walking home in the cold with wet hair, to teach your child a love of the water. Classes meet at the high school pool. Potty-trained kids only please! Please! Swim diapers don't do the trick. Mothers, it's okay to leave your tots with us. We are trained high schoolers who have signed a form swearing we won't flirt with each other and ignore your child, letting him drown.

Adult Night Out! Wooo! Are you ready to rock, Moms and Dads? Then come on down to the VFW Hall for a great night of dancing, spiked punch drinking and scoping out your neighbors for potential affair possibilities. This fun event benefits the high school scholarship fund. Last year two lucky students received $350.00 scholarships to use at the school of their choice. Once again the Pizza Hut will provide all the Dippin' Strips pizza you can eat! Groove to the sounds of LogJam, the rockin' band that played at the fourth of July festivities last summer. (Do you recognize LogJam's bassist? It's Mr. Krenshaw, the middle school's

Biology teacher!) This is an adult-only event…leave the kids with Grandma or a reasonably sober neighbor. Please note: any furtive dope smoking must not take place in the church parking lot next door. Have some respect.

Parents! Many of you have still not signed up for the annual Spruce Up The School Day to be held next Saturday. We still need volunteers to paint the stairwells, weed the butterfly garden and replace the urinal cakes in the boy's bathrooms. Please roll up your sleeves and join in the fun! Let's make our children's school a beautiful place in which to learn/suffer the tauntings of bullies.

Notice! The school cannot be held responsible for any child dropped off before the school day begins at 8:30. We have noticed an increase in this lately, and it is beyond the capacity of the school to supervise these feral children before the first bell rings. So please, no matter how rotten your kid is in the mornings, don't unload him/her on the school before our teachers have had their morning coffee.

Remember To Read! Reading to your child is the best way you can ensure your child's academic success. Read at least fifteen minutes a night, come hell or high water, and mark off the minutes on the detachable I'm A Great Reader! form in back of the monthly newsletter. It is acceptable to make copies of the form if you need more space and are really trying to impress the teachers. Please initial every entry and be sure to have each page notarized. Turn in your form(s) at the end of the month along with your cereal box tops. Your child will get a sticker to wear on his or her shirt which will be forgotten until it shows up mangled in the lint trap of your clothes dryer, and the school gets a dime for every 100 box tops! Together we can change reading from an enjoyable pastime to a dreaded, mandated chore!

PTA-Sponsored lecture: "How To Raise Perfect Kids." Marilyn Guiltmonger, PhD, will speak at the Middle School auditorium Tuesday night at eight. Dr. Guiltmonger is the author of the book *It's Your Fault* and a well-respected educator who was much too busy on the lecture circuit to have children of her own. She will enlighten us about the numerous ways in which we lead our children astray, point out our ham-handed parenting methods/utter ineptitude and give us exercises that will magically correct these issues. Stick around for the question and answer session afterwards…it oughta be good.

Mother's Little Cottage Industries

You can run but you can't hide. There's a party invitation waiting for you in the mailbox. But it's not for just any old party. This is a hideous mutant of a party. At this party you will sit through a presentation about potato peelers or candle snuffers or basket weaving. And then you must buy something or everyone will talk.

Attending these excuses for legalized extortion is part and parcel of modern suburban motherhood. There is no escape if you want to have any form of a social life, and more importantly, nurture the support network you need. So if you buy a lipstick at some mother's Mary Kay party today, you know you can call on that mother to take your kid home from school the day you're laid up with the flu. It's a multi-layered structure of giving and receiving favors more complicated and nuanced than the Mafia's.

Overpriced candles, absurdly ornate scrapbooks, needless kitchenware: I've been to 'em all. I've been in a room with fourteen other women, all dressed in our special "afternoon away from the kids" outfits, and listened to candle experts tell me more about candles than anyone has a right to know. Did you know that if you cut the wick the candle will burn more evenly? And after burning a cylindrical candle you should gently reshape it so it doesn't sag? Well, now I know and so do you. And we're richer for it.

Back in the colonial days women would get together and make a quilt. That was the way they socialized and contributed to the household economy at the same time. Now we sit around comparing knock-off handbags. Yeah, we've come a long way, baby.

I guess some of the stuff is useful, sort of. But some is so over the top it's absurd. How about those baskets … what are they called? Sturm und Drang or Hockaluggie or Ich bin ein Berliner? I forget. But what in the name of all that is sacred can make a freakin' basket cost 75.00? They look exactly the same as the baskets you can pick up at a yard sale for a buck.

Maybe we should brainstorm up some new ideas for house parties. Let's use the current method for success. Take a completely ordinary household item, like a candle, and build an entire industry around it. Create a need for hundreds of related accessories that didn't exist before, and voila! Instant cottage industry.

Let's see ... how about ... a nail file? That's it! We'll start a home party franchise business called "I Want To Nail You" which creates a demand for monogrammed, gemstone-encrusted files you can bring with you anywhere. You really must have the cowhide caddy to carry it in, and the special mineral oil to keep it in good repair. And don't forget the roller brush that whisks away the powdery fingernail residue from your black cocktail dress, thereby saving you from certain social death.

How about those tacky plastic push-pins you've been suffering with all these years? No more! Give a "Stick It!" party and learn about the wonderful world of custom devices designed to enhance your paper-adhering-to-bulletin-board lifestyle. No? Then how about a "Shove It!" party, in which that old, dirty plastic tube from the bank's drive-in lane is replaced with custom tubes you can create yourself and make as unique hostess gifts.

"Suck It!" parties can hawk designer vacuum cleaner bags, "Take Me Out Back And Beat Me Senseless" parties sell fancy egg beaters and whisks, and "Cover Your Ass" parties hawk all kinds of adorable, must-have diaper covers.

Well, anything beats another overpriced Britzkreig Basket.

Recipes for the Rest of Us

I don't know any mothers who find the dopey time-management tips they publish in the mommy mags helpful. If you haven't figured out on your own that you should combine a few errands into one car trip then you're beyond help. Did you know that packing your kids' lunches the night before will make for smoother morning rush hours? Hey, wow, that never occurred to me.

It's also amusing to read the recipes they offer as "Quick and Easy Meals For Families On the Go." What follows is a recipe for Sesame Chicken or Seafood Crepes that lists twenty ingredients. No matter what the recipe is it always calls for fresh cilantro and pine nuts. And we all know how hard it is to keep fresh cilantro and pine nuts in the house. I mean, my kids can't get enough pine nuts, and I'm sure you have the same problem.

I look in my cabinets and I'm inevitably missing at least half the ingredients I would need to make any recipe in the book. I want to see what these kitchen wizards can come up with using the ingredients I actually have on hand at the end of the week:

Five boxes of Jello
A tablespoon of Nutella
Two dented cans of no-salt lima beans I got on sale
Half a bag of Christmas tree-shaped novelty pasta
Three stale marshmallows (Someone forgot to put the Chip Clip back on the bag.)
A can of cream of broccoli soup that I don't even remember buying
"Sweethearts" Valentine candy
A five-pound bag of rice

An unopened L.L. Bean holiday gift pack of assorted flavored coffees
One pound of ground beef with freezer burn
A Batman Pez dispenser and at least twenty refill packs
A smidgen of milk left in the bottom of the gallon jug
A vat of olives from CostCo
A dusty bag of dry lentils leftover from my short-lived frugal phase
A granola bar with one bite missing
A bag with an inch of Tostitos powder at the bottom
Some chopped onion in a Ziploc baggie

Okay, Nigella, Emeril and Martha, what can you do with that? I'd like to see an Iron Chef cook-off. The theme? "Battle: Petrified Gummy Bears."

Stand back and watch the master go to work. Faced with a challenge of this magnitude this is the recipe I would concoct:

First, make yourself a double martini using the olives. Then defrost the ground beef in the microwave. Remove the over-cooked edges and freezer burn. Brown what's left in frying pan. Drain fat. Throw in the Cream of Broccoli soup and what's left of the milk.

Add the chopped onion. Not enough? Surely you have some old onion powder in your spice cabinet! There it is, behind the hot sauce with the X-rated label your neighbors gave you to thank you for getting their mail while they were trying to save their marriage at Couples resort in Jamaica. Break up the dried-out chunks of onion powder between your fingers and add as much as you want. It really doesn't matter.

Let simmer. Add No-Salt lima beans and a teaspoon of salt. Serve the whole mess over the Christmas pasta and tell the kids only five months till Santa comes. If they don't eat it threaten them with lentil soup in their lunchboxes the next day and coal for Christmas. Dessert is Pez-studded Marshmallow Jello with a dollop of Coffee-flavored Nutella and more martinis. Gotta use up those olives.

Quality Shmality

I read a study somewhere that working mothers spend more measurable, one-on-one quality time with their kids than stay-at-home moms do. I didn't react as I suspect the experts would have liked. I guess I should have dropped everything, grabbed my kids away from the clutches of Nickelodeon, and worked with them (in a quality time way) building a drawbridge model out of sugar cubes.

But somehow the study didn't motivate me. Instead, I just got pissed off. I was under the expert's microscope again, an uncomfortable position in which all mothers find themselves today.

Excuse me, but what bastard invented the term "quality time" anyway? I took a long look at the concept and saw it as a huge, smoke-belching guilt factory.

How the hell does one measure quality time? Do the survey-takers actually sit in the room with the mother and child, turning over an egg timer every three minutes? Or do they ask questions over the phone?

Well, there isn't a parent alive, working or not working, that wouldn't lie when asked how much quality time they spend with their children. It's like someone asking you how often you have sex. Are you going to tell the truth and say, "Hmm, I think the last time was Shrove Tuesday, if memory serves"? Or are you going to save face and spout the standard two-to-three times a week response?

I wonder what constitutes quality time in the eyes of the experts. Undivided attention while reading stories to our children? Does it count for more if we read Shakespeare instead of

Captain Underpants? Will we be docked a few points if we have to change a diaper or swat an errant sibling at the same time? Do we have to turn off our cell phones? Does it have to be reading or does watching that cringe-inducing Elmo count too?

What about other activities? Does watching your kid sit on the potty till your eyes cross count as quality time or is that filed somewhere else, like under Wiping, Butts or Training, Potty (See also Hemorrhoids)?

How about grocery shopping? I suppose a quality-time Goody-Two-Shoes would use it as an opportunity to point out the wonderful colors of the eggplants (*aubergines en français, enfants*) and explain the meaning of the phrase *Contents May Settle During Shipping.* I'm afraid I blew it when I gave them all Benedryl and told them to sleep in the cart so we could just get the shopping trip over with.

Maybe there's some kind of definitive ranking system they've developed. Turning your dining room into an ersatz King Arthur's round table and offering to play Merlin would be close to the top. The bottom would be having the cub scouts visit the crystal meth lab in your garage.

Most of us fall somewhere in the middle. That would be the vast, slimy Okeefenokee swampland of guilt, where none of our efforts are good enough, original enough or enriching enough.

Quality Time Nazis will say anything can be a teaching moment. Don't just knock icicles off the roof with a shovel while your darlings play Nintendo. It's a perfect opportunity to talk about stalactite formation. Don't tell them to stop pestering you so you can get dinner ready. That would be a perfect time to go through the spice cabinet, discuss the travels of Marco Polo and assign a writing project researching the origins of cumin. And while we're on the subject, you get mega demerits if you take a Valium while the kids shout "Marco!" "Polo!" at each other in the pool.

How exhausting. I wonder if these experts have any children themselves. If they do I betcha their kids are sitting in front of the tube while Mom or Dad type up their field study results.

I think people read these studies because they want to believe there's a formula for raising children. Just feed the kid organic beets and read to him fifteen minutes a day and it will all turn out dandy. People want guarantees. No one wants to admit that there are none. No one knows anything. A child from the most awful parents can turn out fine. Parents who did everything by the book can easily turn out a monster.

Maybe they should find better research subjects than us poor mothers. Leave us alone. We're tired. We don't want to know how much better everyone else is doing it. It's hard enough. Let us run around our mazes in peace and we'll worry about whether or not the cheese will be there in the end.

Here's a topic the researchers might want to study: How many more times can modern mothers hear about enrichment, quality time and child empowerment before they sock a Child Development Expert in the pie hole? I wouldn't mind being a part of that study, especially if the cage they put me in comes equipped with a wet bar.

Where, Oh Where, Are My Daughters-In-Law?

An interesting idea to me is that, somewhere out there, my future daughters-in-law are wandering about (or sons-in-law, who knows? Hey, if my kid can find true love and someone to remind them to hang up the wet towels I don't care what the plumbing looks like). But for now, I'm assuming my child-in-law will be female.

I scan the little girls' faces around me from time to time, trying to guess if we're passing in the night without knowing it. Is that her, the winsome blonde three-year old in the produce section who is methodically smashing the seedless grapes? Or maybe her, the chubby redhead on the slide, torturing her shell-shocked au pair? (You can tell the poor au pair's wondering how long a way it really is back to Tipperary). No, that's gotta be her over there. She's picking her nose and eating it. A match made in heaven. Welcome to the family, kid.

It was kind of creepy when I realized that someday I would be a mother-in-law. It took a few years for this to dawn on me. It may seem obvious, I know, but I'm not too quick on the uptake these days. Something to do with getting three hours of sleep a night.

I know mother-in-law-ing is a thankless job that has an even lower status and an even greater joke potential than motherhood. I know that you can't win, no matter what. So I'm going to try to stay out of things as much as possible.

Hopefully by the time my children marry I will still be able to remember how I felt and worried when they were young. I'd watch them pick up gum from the sidewalk and chew it before I could stop them, and I wondered how in the hell this barbarian was actually going to grow up to be an independent, functioning adult. Hopefully I will remember the days I despaired of anyone ever falling in love with any of them, considering the fact that they would all fall apart if they weren't the first one to touch the car after racing across the parking lot.

No one will be more shocked than me when I see my darling boys standing up at the altar in their rented tuxes or on the beach in shorts (whatever, I so don't care) waiting for their brides. No one will be more shocked than me if the women actually show up! I'll keep smiling nervously, hoping no one asks whether the groom can tie his own shoes or if he's capable of pouring juice without spilling.

I'll be the first one to leave the reception and skip outta town before anyone's the wiser. Before the groom can complain to his new bride about his best man (one of his brothers) breathing on his dinner roll and now he refuses to eat it. Before he realizes that the wedding cake is not chocolate and has a tantrum.

So if some kind women take my boys off my hands, the last thing I'm going to do is interfere. My boys are their problem now, and I get to have a bubble bath and dance the cha-cha. However they want to stumble thru the bliss of married life and raising children is up to them.

They want to let their son paint his nails…no prob! They want to call my first grandchild Blanket…hey, different strokes!

If they ever do actually ask for advice, I will have none to give anyway. Making a marriage work and raising kids is such an utter mystery to me I would have nothing to offer. All I can tell you is if it's croup, run the hot shower.

Besides, I can't even remember my own kids' baby years. And they're still sort of young. Hell, I'll be lucky if I'm wearing dry panties when I have grandchildren.

Grandchildren. Hmm. I do know what I'll say, however, if they ask me to babysit.

Public Mom vs. Private Mom

Every mother has two sets of parenting skills. One she displays in front of neighbors, strangers and her mother-in-law. The other one she employs when she is home alone with the kids after a long snow day, no milk in the house and a forgotten load of wet laundry left in the washing machine so long it smells like a golden retriever that swam through a stagnant pond.

A friend once mentioned a typical morning for her meant standing in the driveway and yelling at the kids to "just get in the goddamned car already." Then she was horrified to realize that this was the only time her neighbor ever saw her. She allowed her private demon mom to show her pockmarked face in the public mom sphere. This is a common mistake. She won't make it again. Next time she'll make sure her neighbor is on vacation before she performs her morning drama queen routine.

I remember when that sort of thing happened to me. I was in the supermarket parking lot loading groceries into the hatchback while the two boys were beating the stuffing out of each other in the back seat. Finally I *screamed* at them just as two old ladies were passing by the car. They frowned and tsk-tsked me.

Right then I learned a valuable lesson about patience and parenting, and it was this: *if you're going to completely lose your shit and berate your kids until you are hoarse, just make sure you're in the car with the doors closed. Also, tinted windows help.*

We've all made that mistake and I'll wager none of us have forgotten the shame and guilt. It's bad enough to be caught. It's worse when you have to go through the required "I'm a terrible mother" self-flagellation afterwards.

"I can't believe that old lady saw me whack my kid. What kind of a mother whacks her kid? I don't know what I'm doing! I don't even like kids!"

But if we're honest we'll admit that we've all looked over our shoulders before we swat the kid's bum for breaking the Precious Moments statue in the Hallmark store, the one we told him not to touch ten times. If you belong to the No Spanking School, I bet you've used the Vulcan Arm-Grab, the Verbal Abuse or The Fuck-With-The-Kid's-Mind methods instead.

Or how about that teeth-clenched, strained smile Nice Mom voice? That trip to Home Depot when we say, "Darling, if you hide from Mommy in the display bathtub Mommy won't be able to find you and she'll get scared." What we're really thinking is more like "you have no idea how easy it would be for me to leave you here and drive away, so don't pull that stunt again."

When you realize you're being watched you spend a lot of time evaluating other mothers. You try to figure out what you can and can't say in front of them. Can I let down my hair with her or do I have to pretend that I know the name of the school math curriculum? Is she cool, or is she going to rat on me for putting soap on my smart-mouth kid's tongue? What if I tell her it was exfoliating soap instead of Sensitive Skin Dove?

It can be tricky. Some moms I swore were lobotomized Stepford wives turned out to be the most fun. Some hippie-dippie types I thought were okay turned out to be members of the Parenting Division of the KGB.

The gulags are full of mothers like us who said the wrong thing, just once. Like all mothers who have screwed up in public I live in fear of the van of thugs coming to get me under the cover of darkness. But then again, how hard can it be to break rocks in a prison camp after hosting a birthday party for twenty one year olds? *You want a piece of me, Stalin? Do realize I was up all night stuffing goodie bags? Bring on the sledgehammer, Koba.*

This division between the informant moms and the cool moms became evident one afternoon. My son had his buddy over to play. The kids had been fine but I was not having a good day. I was questioning everything from why I even had kids to why I didn't take off a year to backpack around Europe when I was twenty-two and now it's too damn late.

I was in a mood. My hair was a mess. I had been trying for some sort of look but gave up and was sucked back into baseball cap hell. I was wearing Regulation Momwear: jeans and sweat-shirt, in desperate need of some tweezing, no make-up. These days, if I don't wear my under-eye cover-up spackle my friends think I'm looking to hit them up for money. I look that good.

So the mom showed up to pick up her kid and said, "Gosh you look tired. Are you okay?" What a dweeb. I should have known right then that she was an informant. I mean, what mother tells another mother that she looks tired? We're ALL tired ALL the time. It's like pointing out that the grass is green, for fuck's sake.

Forcing a chuckle, I told her I was just having a bad day and wanted to run away from home. The usual "let's make light of this and laugh" repartee. But she took me at face value and stood there with her mouth open. Later she mentioned to other mothers that she was worried about me!

I started getting concerned calls from other moms in town, thinking I was on the brink of pulling a Sylvia Plath. And I thought I was putting on a brave face! Good thing I didn't tell her that I had just gotten a tattoo and was considering selling my kids on e-Bay with the *Buy It Now!* option activated.

So no matter how rotten your kids behave keep that Evil Mom locked up in the attic with a wig and a rocking chair. And beware of the informants. Now that you know they're out there keep an eye out for these types: Those old folks who forgot how hard it is to raise kids and only remember the sweet things like choo-choo footie pajamas. The childless couples on their way to a quiet restaurant meal who look on aghast as you comically maneuver the double stroller while juggling cups of cheerios and vats of diaper wipes. Even the other mothers you thought you could trust may squinting at you and whispering into their Mother's Day corsages/mini walkie-talkie.

You're probably being watched even as you read this. Don't look up! Just dredge up those Nice Mom skills that you use in public. Refer to yourself in the third person and say things like "hurry, darling, Mumsy doesn't want you to be late for Kinder-Richment!" Fight the urge to say "for the love of Pete, move! I'm going to light a fire under you if you don't pick up the pace, sloth-boy!"

Despite all your precautions you may accidentally expose your private mom skill set in front of the wrong people. If one night you find yourself handcuffed in the back of a prison van with a blanket over your head, don't despair. We can room together in Shawshank.

Consistency In Discipline

When my oldest was a baby, I used to sing (very badly, but he didn't care) "Sweet Baby James" to him, over and over till he fell asleep. I was flush with the excitement and fatigue of new motherhood. I must have been, because I hate "Sweet Baby James."

I haven't thought about that for a few years until the other day I was standing in my kitchen and that song happened to play on the radio. Instantly I was transported back over the years and I was a blubbering mess. I yearned to hold my grown-up baby and right about then he appeared in the kitchen. A tall, skinny sixth-grader, all arms and legs and teeth and freckles, my darling, the love of my life, standing before me…*with a rotten scowl on his face.* "WHY do I have to practice piano. I'm NOT going to do it. It's stupid, and you can't make me."

The shitty 'tude he's been sporting lately snapped me out of my tearful reverie and I felt much better. Things were back to normal. I scowled back at my darling miracle and said "Don't push me, buster, if you want to see your Nintendo DS again" or something to that effect.

Back in the days when I knew how to parent, before I had kids, I would hear a kid mouthing off to his parents and think "I will never allow MY child to speak to me that way."

Well, usually I don't. But sometimes I have. I know I should be consistent but usually I'm too damn tired. In an instant I'm supposed to remember the same punishment I imposed in the past for the same offense? I can't do that, especially when I'm trying to back out of my driveway in the dark and trying to answer my youngest's earnest question about aliens at the same time. Was the punishment no Gameboy or no Cartoon Network? Did I even say anything at all or did I give him a size nine in the keister?

It gets much more complicated when you throw some more kids into the mix because every mother knows you're tougher on the first. The baby can be swallowing swords and you'll mumble "just don't scratch the new countertop, OK?."

We all start out thinking we have it nailed. We refuse to retrieve the thrown sippy cup after ten tosses, no matter how loudly the baby screams. There, that's setting limits! What's the big deal? I'm SO on top of this consistency thing!

Things get fuzzy later on. One day you'll be stuck: the only way you're going to be able to find time to clean before a dinner party is to ship the kids next door. You know, the neighbors whose parenting skills make yours look like T. Berry Brazelton's. The kids may become experts at playing Grand Theft Auto, but at least you'll have a clean house. Consistency? Right. You're going to find yourself in more compromising positions than Paris Hilton.

Then there's the whole potty mouth thing. I really want to be one of those moms whose kids could eat at Buckingham Palace. I want to be a mom who looks aghast when her son belches at the table and demands an immediate "excuse me." I want to be the mom who demands a certain decorum, a certain level of manners worthy of the station in life to which my children should ascend.

But, let's face it. I will not be surprised at all when they do a boardinghouse reach for the scones at high tea. I know they'll be singing the "penis penis penis" song they just made up or having a farting contest in front of the Queen.

I've tried to be consistent with this, but I'm the worst offender. I can let a belch rip with the best of them, and my salty tongue is legendary in these parts. So I suppose I want them to be well-mannered gentlemen in front of everyone else, and good ol' slobbos at home. How's that for consistency?

Now Play Nice with the Other Mommies

God, I hate this part of motherhood. I have to go to a "meet and greet" coffee with all the other Preschool mommies. Most alienated stay-at-home moms would welcome the chance at adult conversation flavored with sugary snack foods, but not me. Being an antisocial loser, facing these school events makes me want to hide behind the couch, pull the throw from Target over my head and shout 'SON? I HAVE NO SON!'

I'm just not a graceful partygoer. I always think of the time the whole office went out for Japanese, everyone took off his or her shoes at the restaurant, and I was the only one with a hole in my sock. I just know it's going to suck and it's going to be awkward.

What could be so bad, you say. Oh, I don't know. Nothing in particular, I guess. It's just that when I'm stuck in a room with twenty chirping, Lily-Pulitzer-wearing mothers discussing the virtues of Miss Muff's Mommy and Me Music class, I just short-circuit. I start to twitch. The gargantuan effort I need to put in just so I appear to be a normal, medicated suburban mother like everyone else leaves me exhausted and in dire need of a double Jack Daniel's. Neat, please.

If I don't attend today's coffee my son will likely be excluded from all the playdates. I don't want to punish my son for my own social clutziness, so I have to go and talk the talk. I have to act like I give a shit that their little Parker is in the 95th percentile for height AND weight, but his sister is only in the 25th.

I've been to so many of these little events that I know what the refreshments will be before I get there. A Crudite platter with

Ranch dressing, for starters. The "western front" Weight Watchers moms will nibble on raw carrots, while the "eastern front" Atkins moms load up on provolone from the antipasto dish. There will be a cookie platter (the de-militarized zone) from the local bakery.

I pull up to the gorgeous, graceful home, complete with the custom iron address marker and the brass faux saddlebag mailbox. I park my muddy, dented minivan amongst the immense, gleaming SUV's. The scene looks like Rose of Sharon, the toothless Cracker, just showed up at the debutante cotillion sporting acid-washed jeans and curling-ironed bangs. Taking a bit of perverse pride in my choice of wheels, and assuming much more of an air of populist environmental superiority than I deserve, up to the house I go.

I've got my game face on. I spot the beautiful hostess and say my hellos. She greets me pleasantly enough. For some reason I notice her impeccable cuticles as she offers her hand. Clearly, Soft Scrub is not part of her manicure routine. I hope my own shredded cuticles don't scrape her. Maybe it's time to bring back little white gloves.

I go into the dining room to fill out my nametag (warning sign #1). Within seconds another mom makes a bee-line for me and tells me that she noticed on the class roster that her son has a birthday the same week as my son, and have I decided yet what treats I'll be sending in on my son's birthday, because her son has allergies, you see, not to peanuts, but he has soy and egg white "issues," and could I let her know what the treats will be so she can tell me if it's safe for her son, because her son misses out on so much, and she really doesn't want him to miss out, although he's getting really good at asking people what the ingredients are, but you never know with people, and he'll just throw up right away if he eats the wrong thing, so do I know what the treats will be?

I just blink for a second or two, and say "uh ... cupcakes?" Okay, that's fine, are you baking from scratch or using a mix, because some brands of mixes are okay, if you use Duncan Hines that should be fine, and Duncan Hines frosting is okay too. "Well, Duncan Hines it is then." Oh good, that's great, because I wouldn't want him to miss out ...

I back away and watch as she attacks another mom and I'm let off the hook. Ignoring gasps from the dieting moms I grab a cookie. Munching away, I admire the regulation dark red dining room without a single dirty diaper or dusty Cap'n Crunch nugget poking out from under the server (warning sign #2). Suddenly we are ordered into the living room because "we have business to discuss." Gulp. Last time I heard that from a skinny, waspy woman I was about to get fired.

Turns out she wanted to discuss the Class Present Protocol. Who knew this was such an urgent matter? It's only September. I just assumed everyone was like me, scuttling around Odd Job in dark glasses, buying discontinued gift-boxed chocolates on December 24th. I guess that's why my life looks the way it does and Waspy's life looks the way hers does.

Suddenly depressed, I listen in as the discussion begins. Should we take a collection now that will cover all the teacher gifts for the year, or should we leave it up to the individual? The matter is debated at lightening speed. Ideas are thrown out for discussion and crushed flatter than a Kate Spade bag under a Hummer's wheels.

I'm speechless. After a full sixty seconds the floor is closed. It's decided that exactly $50.00 will be collected from each mom that will be used as cash presents for the teachers at Christmas and at the end of the school year. I must say these women are efficient, if a bit lacking in the spontaneous warmth department.

Business complete, the group then coagulates into little subsets. And as usual I'm the only one in mine: the null set. Little snippets of conversation float above the din and I can occasionally understand a few of them. Sort of like when a group of people is speaking French and I can pick out the words "le blue jean" and "merde."

I hear about how little Meghan LOVES gymnastics, just LOVES it. I hear the mom with the Argentine accent describing her son's dirty knees, or maybe it's her pet Pekinese. I hear about a great ballet class for boys (warning sign #3), and then how someone needed a brand new stove just because a turkey wouldn't fit in it. Hmm. That's a problem? Sounds like a great way to get out of hosting Thanksgiving, missy.

The crowd chirps on. To my surprise I realize that I'm actually enjoying this little gathering. One good thing about being socially awkward is that you get to stand back and observe. In doing this I realize why everyone except me is so excited: this is the first taste of this crapola. For them this is the first time a child is in school, even if it is only preschool, and it's all a wonderland of fun and learning.

I know. I was in their shoes once. I remember it felt so good to talk to other adults after being chained to the house during the endless baby years. But by the time your third one gets to preschool, your older kids are headed towards junior high. School has become a nine-month long babysitting service that cranks out endless forms to fill out and demands you construct rain-forest dioramas the night before they are due. The romance is gone.

You also begin to realize, with a bit of perspective, how little of this whole preschool experience really matters in the end. It just doesn't pay to blow your wad now getting whipped up about the too-small cubbies or the fact that the Afternoon Two's have to wait till next year to start Spanish class. Save it for the big fights later. You're going to need your strength.

You learn pretty quickly that you better pace yourself socially as well because you're going to be going to hundreds of these events over the years. It's one of those things they don't tell you in *What to Expect When You're Expecting.*

The ovulation predictor kits should come with a package insert: "WARNING! Just so you can't say no one warned you, you are embarking on a career of going to coffees, squeezing your butt into tiny chairs at Back To School Nights, and looking under couch cushions for pencils so your kids can do homework. If you're not ready for this, there's a sale on condoms over in aisle three. Put down this item, back away slowly, then turn and run. Run!"

Finally the gathering ends. We say our good-byes, promising to call to schedule playdates (ugh) and with the phone number of that wonderful woman who makes custom crib quilts. Thrilled at being set free, I practically skip out of there. I know I will forget most of these women's names by the time I get back to the car, but please God, don't let me forget one thing when it's time to buy that cupcake mix: Duncan Hines! Duncan Hines!

A "New and Improved" "Zagat's For Parents"

Restaurant reviews actually used to matter to me, back in the days when I could get out to dinner whenever I flipping well felt like it. But now I'm a mother and, well, you parents know how things change. Now 'Nobu' sounds to us like the toddler's valiant effort at pronouncing "no boots." Any parent knows "The Four Seasons" are Back To School, Holiday Toy Shopping, Summer Camp and Thank God The Kids Can Finally Play Outside. But Zagat's guides are written in a handy, easy-to-use format, so perhaps we could use the Zagat's formula for reviews of places that are relevant to us now. For example:

The Playground by the Soccer Field

This playground is fenced in but has "only one overripe porta-john for a bathroom" so if you're kid is potty-training "forget it." There's a "bird poop-encrusted tire swing" and it's crowded on Saturdays with "divorced dads who have their kids visiting." Don't go on hot days because then "the mulch they put down really stinks." Watch out for "teens having sex in the covered slide" unless you're prepared to have "the talk." Beware of the "undisciplined tough kids hogging the baby slide," and the "gossiping throng of nannies" on the benches too busy to notice their charges' rotten behavior. But the playground is "next to the train tracks" so your little boy can "watch trains go by till his brains fall out." It's also next to the public basketball courts so be prepared to hear some language that "will really curl your m*****f***in' hair. Ya know what I'm sayin', dog?"

The McDonald's on the Highway

This McDonald's tables aren't as filthy as the ones up at the mall food court, but "the johns are worse" so make sure your kids "pee before you go." They are "always out of the big kid Happy Meal Hot Wheels toys" so your fourth-grader will probably get "stuck with a Teletubbies keychain." The help is only "mildly surly," but the fellow diners "tend toward the cretinous." At all costs "avoid the fun zone," as the ball pit "reeks of urine" and the glass windows turn it into a "greenhouse/petri dish of rhinovirus culture." Naturally, there is the "regulation fat kid" who is "way too old" for the ball pit, and will be sure to bully your child. He's always there, so he must be a "McDonald's employee on an extended break." If you must go or your kid will have a "total shitfit," be sure to bring a change of clothes and a plastic bag as the "vomit aroma" will cling to your darling for hours.

Elm Street Sidewalks

This block is generally flat enough to push a stroller on comfortably, except for the sidewalk in front of number forty-six, as there's a "insane cat lady" who lives there and "her sidewalk is potholed." At number fifty-two, beware of the "crazed, ankle-biting Scottie" who lurks in the "boxwood shrub." Bring along your preschooler, who will love the "novelty backhoe mailbox" and "creepy garden gnomes" at number thirty-nine. "Whatever you do avoid number sixteen" unless you have "an hour to kill" chatting with the "colorful, twitching Vietnam Vet" about the township committee and conspiracy theories. Cross to the other side and "pray he's too drunk to see you." As you near Pine Street beware of the old slate sidewalks that have "buckled like the San Andreas fault." You just may slam into one of these and send your child flying out of the stroller "like a boulder from a catapult."

The Local Warehouse Store

There is "no good time" to come here, "only bad and worse" times. Even if you're the first one in at opening time, and you buzz through the store, your "hopes of a quick escape will be dashed" as there will be "only one cashier open" with a line ten carts deep. Avoid the toilet paper displays. "No one needs 64 rolls" unless one is an Osmond or a Kennedy, and it "takes up too much room" in your cart. Instead "hurry straight toward the personal products aisle." Put the "gross of tampons and Compound W" at the bottom of your cart. You can cover it up in the next aisle with the "vat of ranch dressing" thereby saving embarrassment. "Stay clear of the clothing." That seemingly "cute bargain sweater" will "morph into old lady clothing" on the way home, and you know you'll never get around to returning it. If you must bring your kids, go around lunchtime. Casually breeze past the "free samples of cooked sausage, cheese puffs and corndogs." Bring along a wig for disguise so "you can sneak seconds." With practice you can "feed your kids lunch while you shop" and "kill two birds with one stone."

The Supermarket

The supermarket that was "featured on *Sixty Minutes* for changing meat expiration dates" is convenient, and "doesn't smell as bad as it used to." The "carts tend to stick together," but the challenge of separating them provides a "satisfying diversion" as well as "much-needed exercise." The potato bread by the front door is a "good deal," but stay away from the "scary chocolate-covered jelly rings." Head right to the fresh veggies. If you're lucky "the misters will come on while you bag green beans," giving the kids a thrill. Your kids will also love "sticking their fingers into the plastic-wrapped ground beef." Luckily "the candy aisle is right there" so you can get them lollipops to "shut them the hell up." You can usually find some "tuna on sale for 99 cents," and at the end of aisle twenty there's always a "good deal on detergent," but you have to dig past the "sad little knock-off Barbie display." By now the lollipops are gone so "get right to the checkout." Go to the one on the end with "the *Star* magazine that's torn but still readable." The "raptor-taloned cashiers" are "pure evil," so "don't even try" to make small talk. Read about Jessica and Nick in the *Star* as your kids "re-arrange the Lifesaver display." When you're done "maneuver past the Senior Citizens Bus" blocking the door, while "avoiding the crabby seniors." "Catch the eggs" as they fall out of the bag. When you get home wash your hands, since more colds are transmitted by "revolting shopping cart handles" than anything else.

The PTA meeting

Don't go on budget nights. Try to "sit near the back" for quick escapes. Whatever you do, "don't sign up for anything." If they pressure you, "tell them to call you next week." If that doesn't work, just say you can "make cupcakes for the bake sale." Never, repeat, "never volunteer for lunchroom supervision duty." You don't want to know what goes on in there. If there's a guest speaker "bring along a good book." If you see a friend "don't sit next to her." You'll be shushed for whispering to each other. Wait until tomorrow to "compare gossip about the real nut-job moms." Sprinkle your conversation with terms like "curriculum and phonics" so it "looks like you know what you're talking about." If you're asked to "comment on needed improvements to the school," bring up the "terrible condition of the boys' bathroom." You "can't go wrong" with that one.

Home Depot

See if you can "grab one of those huge rolling cart thingys" so the kids can have a ride. If the "orange vest gestapo" stops you at the door just say "you need the cart because you're buying lumber." Might as well pick up a box of "60 watt light bulbs"; why the hell not? Hoping to spot an orange vest to help you is "like *Waiting for Godot*," so amuse the kids in the plumbing department by letting them "sit on the display toilets." Be prepared to explain to the kids "the difference between potty and putty" amid "guffaws from the kids" and disapproving looks from other "hopelessly lost, aimlessly wandering customers." Once you finally find the drawer for the screws you need "it will be empty." No matter what time you go to the store "the express register will be closed." You will be forced to "wait behind the compulsive price checker" who demands the cashier call over the manager. Pay for the light bulbs at last. If you get to the parking lot without "losing one of your kids in the storm door section," consider yourself lucky. If you realize "you forgot the sandpaper," which is what you went there for in the first place, "go home and call a contractor."

Kiddie Product Hall of Shame

Lego, I hate you. Don't pull that "it's educational" crap on me. Educational for parents, maybe, since we're the ones who wind up assembling the stuff.

I have a question for you. Can you possibly cram a few thousand more pieces into your next series of Star Wars Jedi fighters or whatever they are? And surely you can make them even smaller than you do now.

Also, it was a great idea you guys had about making your boxes un-resealable! Tiny pieces fall out of the corners and ends. I'll bet you can make the pieces sharper too. That way, when we step on them with bare feet at night, they will really lacerate instead of merely bruise.

I also enjoy this feature: some of the pieces hold together so well a crowbar can't separate them, while the integral parts fall off easily. Harry Potter Lego goes around without his head; Chewbacca has no legs.

Wait a second, all of you over there in the Thomas/Brio factory. I hear you laughing but I haven't forgotten you price-gouging bastards. It's pretty funny to charge $15.00 for two pieces of wooden track, huh? Even funnier that we all actually buy it. Damn, I wish I woulda thought of that!

Hey, Hot Wheels! I remember when you made cars and pieces of orange track. That was it. Back then playing with Hot Wheels at least involved some form of creativity, because the kids could design their own track layouts. But one of you geniuses came up with the idea of creating complete boxed "playsets." The Hot Wheels Car Wash, or Monster Truck Jam or whatever. The kids can't put it together, lose interest in it after fifteen minutes, and you get to charge a lot more for it. Brilliant!!

Same thing with you Barbie people. We had Barbie and Midge and Ken and Skipper. We changed the clothes only. Now if the kids want a new outfit, they buy a new doll too! I've got to hand it to you marketing people.

Hey, Stride-Rite! You've positioned yourself as the shoe brand responsible parents choose. You charge fifty bucks for a pair of size one sneakers and mom walks away thinking she's given her kid the best start in life, podiatry-wise.

But that's not enough. You proclaim we can't hand the shoes down to our other kids, because that will turn their feet into hideous, useless appendages. Frightened, we buy more shoes for fifty bucks a pair, thinking we are paying for the professional fitter's expertise.

No way. I'm not buying that nonsense anymore. How hard is it to push your thumb on the toe and make sure there's some room there? I can do that. And I can do it at K-Mart, too, with shoes that cost 80% less. Guess what? I handed down shoes three times over, and none of my kids are limping or forced to walk on their hands.

So all of you…consider yourselves outed!

The First Full Day of Summer Vacation, or, How Long Can 24 Hours Feel?

6:30: My husband rumbles to life but I lie in bed half-awake, vaguely aware that this morning feels different. I don't have the mental capacity at this caffeine-challenged hour to fathom what the reason could possibly be. Sod it, I'm going back to sleep. This is heaven! I should be able to snooze for another half-hour. Or at least until the children park themselves next to my bed holding out their cereal bowls.

6:32: My five-year-old crawls in for a cuddle. So much for my nap. Yes, he's darling, but can't he wait till seven o'clock to exhibit all his charms?

6:45: A few prods in the chops from bony little elbows force me to abandon my tribute to sloth. I should get going. Lunches to make. Are there any cheesefood slices left? I have to remember to scour out that lunchbox so the drosophila stop propagating in it. Dammit, I'm out of juice boxes. And all the water bottles leak.

6:47: Hey, wait! Today is the first day of summer vacation! I don't have to make any lunches! No schlepping for me today!

6:47:15: But what am I going to do with them all day? Strange, even though yesterday was the last day of school I was in denial. I could sort of forget that I had two and a half months of 24/7 Quality Time ahead of me to endure.

7:00: *"Can we play video games?"*

7:15: *"We're hungry!"*

7:45: *"Mom, can you get up and come downstairs? Skippy spilled the orange juice!"*

7:45:30: I wipe up the orange juice and clean up the breakfast mess. I don't know what's worse, making their breakfast or letting them do it and cleaning up afterwards. I make my coffee and slump over the paper with my caffeine drip and tell them to leave me alone.

8:30: Ah, that's better. I'm alive now. Hmm, wonder where the kids are?

8:40: I finally find them playing video games. I make the usual lame threat to throw the Goddamn Game Cube™ out the window, but they know I'm just whistling in the wind. They know I need it for free babysitting like a junkie needs a fix. They yawn and shuffle dejectedly out of the room. "Go outside and play!" *"It's raining."* "Well, go find something to do."

8:45: *"Mom, can we make a cyclone experiment? We saw it on Zoom."* Damn. I can't think of a good reason to say no and they sense my weakness, like hyenas surrounding a lame antelope.

I fish a couple of two-liter bottles out of the recycling, unearth some electric tape from the mountain of crap on my husband's workbench, and find a bottle of food coloring after emptying out my spice cabinet. We build the contraption but despite my best efforts it leaks blue water all over the place.

The kids give up and go back to visiting Mario and Luigi, while I scour the blue food coloring drops out of the countertop. *Damn you, Zoom! Damn you, Durkee Food Coloring!*

9:00: Now what?

9:01: I decide we need a schedule. This lollygagging about is not good for the children. How will they ever adjust to being back in school come September after running wild all summer like so many feral cats? I jump on the computer and make up a Chore Chart and an allowance payment schedule.

When I show the kids they are surprisingly receptive. They make their beds, unload the dishwasher and take out the garbage, eager to make check marks on the chart. I stand there disbelieving and watch them with my head cocked to the side like a dog who hears a funny noise.

10:00: *"We're hungry!*

"You may have an apple or a banana."

"Why can't we have gummy bears?"

"Because *Child* magazine said that if I stock up on healthy treats you would gleefully lunge for them. Didn't you kids read the article?"

10:30: I pile everyone into the car to go sign up for the Summer Reading Program at the library.

I don't know what I've done wrong but my kids hate to read. I've done everything the experts said to do.

I read to them till I began shouting "Do you like my hat? Yes, I like that party hat!" to stunned passersby. The children see me reading constantly, everything from the *Times* to *People* to Camus. That's called modeling proper behavior, right T. Berry?

But when I mention that we're going to the library they react like I'm asking them to watch paint dry.

"It's BOR-ing."

"How can it be boring? There's a wonderland of imagination waiting for you!"

They roll their eyes and get in the car.

"We're going and you'll learn to like reading if I have to break every bone in your bodies."

10:45: There are gaggles of children happily reading, tra-la, nestled in every nook and cranny of the children's room. *"Look, Mommy, a new book by Jamie Lee Curtis! Let's read it together, then dance around the maypole and toss rose petals about!* What the hell?

My kids shuffle in as if they're facing the executioner. I try to get them enthused.

"Look at the prizes you can win!"

Then I take a closer look at the prizes. I must admit they're pretty lame. Four hours of reading and all you get is a paper animal to color? Sixteen hours for a bouncy ball? Whoop dee doo. But I hide my disappointment.

"Look at what you get for 150 hours!!! A yoyo!"

They sulk. That's what's wrong with kids nowadays. They don't know how to yoyo.

12:00: I decide to take them out to lunch at the diner in town. I walk out twenty-five dollars poorer. Note to self: *Suck it up and make more PBJ's at home or else you're going to have to get a real job.*

1:15: Seeing that I blew big bucks at lunch I figure I'll get out the clippers and give them their summer buzzcuts. That's fifty bucks I'll save by not going to the barber. Think what that'll buy at Target! And the human hair flying around the backyard will keep the deer out of my neighbor's garden. He should thank me.

2:00: Desperate, I call a few of their friends over to play. They all promptly disappear in front of the Goddamn Gamecube again. I shoo them outside. I check on them a few minutes later. One boy is hitting a tree with a baseball bat. The other is hitting the sandbox top with a golf club. Another is kicking woodchips from the flowerbed onto the lawn. The rest are taking turns yawning.

"Hey kids! How about some tag or something?"

"That's boring."

2:45: *"Mom, can you set up the slip and slide?"* Normally taking on a project like this would be only slightly more palatable than getting a complete Brazilian wax, but today I'm out of better ideas.

3:15: Blue-lipped and dizzy from blowing up the damn thing, I stumble over to the hose to turn it on. Thank God it works. I run upstairs to look for bathing suits. Now, where did I put them for the winter? Ah, yes, under the bed. A bit dusty, so what. They'll get clean in the water. Then I hear the tell-tale crinkling of dried out, useless waistband elastic. The kids wind up mooning the whole neighborhood with every pass down the slip and slide.

I wonder what the new mom across the street must be thinking as she watches the two or three hundred boys hurtling themselves across my lawn as I sit slumped in my white resin lawn chair drinking a Bud Lite.

5:00: The kids' friends go home. I decide to go to the town pool to pick up our pool badges, the keys to a summer chock full of Marco Polo and Athlete's Foot. Waiting in line with other scantily-clad people in bathing suits, I decide I'm seeing way too much of my neighbors.

6:00: Dinnertime. Hmm, what to make? Large pie, half pepperoni, deliver it please. I'll throw them some grapes to ease the guilt and cut the grease.

7:00: "*Can we play video games?*"

8:00: Time for bed. Hop to it, troops! You're tired, I can tell.

9:30: I said go to bed! I told you that you were tired! Now get to bed. Please?

9:32: My husband comes home after working a late night. He asks what I did all day.

"Nothing," I say.

I don't have the mental energy to go into the myriad details, and even if I did his eyes would glaze over as he feigned interest. He goes upstairs to kiss the children goodnight and gets them all amped up again in the process. It goes from *All Quiet on the Western Front* to *The Good, The Bad and the Ugly* within seconds.

I don't intervene. He started it so he can deal with it. After a few more minutes I hear him raise his voice. "Settle Down!"

He comes back downstairs and slumps onto the sofa next to me. "Wow, they're a handful!"

No shit.

10:00: Ah, alone time. They're finally asleep. I curl up with a good book and reflect. After a day like this even the editors of *Family Fun* magazine would throw up their hands in defeat and start counting the minutes till school starts again. But I'll get through the summer okay if I can just get this little respite at night to read and think about something other than children.

10:02: Asleep on couch.

Back-To-School "Momku"

No-show volunteers.
Hell hath no fury like a
dissed PTA mom.

Look into yourself.
The patience you seek is there.
Second grade class play.

Do not rest just yet.
Once more you will take that ride.
Forgotten lunch box.

Last minute panic.
Permission slip is due.
Must have been thrown out.

Hold fast to knowledge.
What do you mean you can't find
your library book?

Everything kids need
they get in Kindergarten,
like rhinovirus.

Back in the old days
All lunchboxes were either
"Campus Queen" or Plaid.

Score a brand-new fleece
while cleaning the Lost and Found.
Finders Keepers, kid.

Traveling sports teams.
Long games in far-away towns.
Kiss weekends goodbye.

What's more unlikely?
Saving enough for college
or seeing pigs fly?

Do not ask for whom
the bell tolls…it tolls for you.
Late to school again.

God saves a special
place in heaven for Moms who
chaperone class trips.

School says keep kid home
a full day after fever
but how will they know?

September at last.
The kids walk sadly to school
but Mom does a jig.

"Help me with homework!"
You thought you were done with school?
You have just begun.

Whole language? Phonics?
The debate rages onward
Bring back Dick and Jane.

The awesome amount
of flyers sent home from school
can make Greenpeace weep.

PTA Nazis
search for moms who volunteer.
Don't give them your name!

"Can you chaperone?
Will you chair a committee?"
Go-run away fast!

Waning summer brings
the autumnal rite...new socks,
Haircut and undies.

By September first,
spending time with the children
seems overrated.

I don't understand.
They must be stark-raving mad.
How do they home-school?

Ah...steaming coffee
never tasted so good as
on day one of school.

Must have new crayons.
Old pencils not good enough.
School supply racket.

If fighting were a
subject in school, all siblings
would be A students.

Tears, clinging, long hugs.
Are the kids sad? No, it's the
Kindergarten moms.

For Mom, no Porsche can
compare to the sight of a
big yellow schoolbus.

Bully said SpongeBob
is for dorks? Well, let him buy
you a new backpack.

How was your first day?
Teacher mean. Too much homework.
Ugh. Long year ahead.

Kid...here's a secret:
you'll never use Algebra.
It's all a big lie.

"What's a vagina?
Some kid said it at recess."
Gulp: time for The Talk.

Summertime, and the
living is easy? Yeah, right.
Gershwin had no kids.

The words just roll off
your tongue: arabica bean.
Mother's salvation.

Somebody Gave My Kid A Chemistry Set

There it was, in the pile of birthday gifts we brought home from the FunPark Party Room. A goddamn chemistry set. I don't know who gave this present to my kid, but when I find out there will be hell to pay. That kid's parents will rue the day they regifted that chemistry set to my son as they deal with tiny Puzz 3D foam pieces stuck in their fancy rugs.

I tried to hide it before my kids saw it, but no luck. Naturally it's the first thing they wanted to try out. "Mom, can you help us?" Oh boy. There's nothing I'd rather do. I spread out the newspaper on the kitchen counter and attempt to read the directions.

"Mom, it says here we need plastic clothespins, ordinary white household glue, magnets in assorted sizes, toilet paper cores, ball bearings, safety pins, pipe cleaners, ordinary household table salt, staples and a piece of cardboard from a shirt box. Do we have any of that stuff?"

"Um, we have salt."

"Mommmmm!"

Alright, alright. Jeez, give me a minute, I'm thinking. What's the matter with me? How come I hate this stuff? This is the kind of quality time opp that I stayed home for in the first place. What kind of a mother would I be if I squashed their quest for knowledge?

I suck it up and begin my search for the various components. I detach my homeowners' insurance and house deed in order to harvest the staples. I unroll a brand new toilet paper roll to get to the core and I smash a *"Greetings From Stone Mountain, Georgia"* refrigerator magnet with a truncheon to isolate the actual magnet embedded within.

"Hey, kids! Where are you? I found all the stuff you need! Kids?"

I find them on the computer playing the farting Santa clip on JibJab and screaming with laughter. They don't even hear me. I get right up to their faces.

"Hey, what about the experiment? Remember the chemistry set?" "Huh? Oh, maybe later."

"Oh, no way, darlings. I just peeled off wallpaper to scrape some glue off the back since that was on the list of required ingredients, so we will be doing that little experiment NOW."

Sulking, everyone plods down to the kitchen counter, where the experiment will fail miserably. The kids then retreat to the TV room to digest their newly-gleaned scientific knowledge in front of a SpongeBob rerun. I'm left with the mess to clean up. And also with a lame hope that they will remember their dear Mother always had time for them and their whims, had all the materiel at the ready and always encouraged learning.

They had better.

Warped Values: Only $12.50 Per Child, Cake Included!

When did children's birthday parties become more elaborate than the Trooping of the Color?

Birthday parties have nothing to do with kids anymore. It's all about the parents showing off and pretending they're doing it in the name of Fun.

I've been to countless catered, well-planned preschool birthday parties and nobody has any Fun. Unless there's an open bar in the kitchen, that is. Whatever happened to Pin-The-Tail and warm Kool-Aid?

Pick up any of those magazines that are free for the taking at the pediatrician's office or the preschool, like *Mommy Guilt* or *Parenting Pressure.* Check out the classifieds. The dizzying array of birthday party choices available can make your head spin. Should you hire a petting zoo, a starving actor dressed up as Spiderman, a moonwalk? Are two-year-olds too young for ballroom dance lessons? *This is crazy,* you think. *I'll just have a few kids over for musical chairs.*

Good luck bucking the trend! If your child has been invited to every birthday party you too must invite the entire preschool class. Don't forget siblings, cousins and neighbors as well. Unless you live on the Disney Cruise ship you'll soon be looking for a Fun Place to have the party.

If one can quantify folly and charade these Fun Places would rank right up there with Catherine the Great's tour through Russia. Happiness is paraded before you and misery is hidden behind the happy serfs making balloon animals.

The worst is Chuck E. Cheese. There's something about an

ex-felon wearing an enormous papier-mache mouse head that gives me the creeps. It's our fate to be mothers in the age of vomit-encrusted plastic tube mazes and piss-scented ball pits.

I still shudder when I think about my last trip across the River Styx for my son's friend's birthday party. I watched in horror as a child rifled through the sticking pyramid of socks by the ball pit, trying to find his own. He methodically sniffed each one until he somehow found his own particular note of foot odor.

I looked around to see if any other parent noticed so we could share a "did you just see that?" commiserating glance. But all the other parents were walking around dazed, struggling to find a happy place they could go to in their heads in order to endure this waking nightmare.

Grossed out by Chuck E. Cheese? Then consider renting a party room in your local ersatz children's museum. You know the type of place: someone gets hold of an old fire truck and a sand table and hangs out a shingle. Recently I was forced to drag my son to a party at one of these florescent-lit mini-hells.

The cacophony of screaming children and the blasting loud choruses of "Baby Beluga" instantly made me put on my "Let Me Just Get Through This" face. I looked at my watch, calculating the earliest possible socially acceptable time to split. I had ninety minutes to kill.

Trying to make the best of it, my son and I became absorbed by the "Make Your Own Moon Crater" table. This involved dropping a rubber ball into a vat of baking powder. I was mesmerized. Finally, I looked up and noticed my son had wandered off.

I joined the clusterfuck of parents asking "have you seen Cody? Cassidy? Cara? Caitlin?" A blaring loudspeaker shattered my trance. "*Will the friends and family of…* **Connor**… *please* *report to Party Room Number Seven to sing Happy Birthday to...* **Connor**!"

I found my son in Party Room Number Seven eating his endangered species animal crackers and trying his best with the accompanying educational activity. *Hey kids! Help Koko find her way out of the Jungle Maze before the poacher sees her!* All items were conveniently provided by a birthday decoration catalog. I guess **Connor** has a fetish for mountain gorillas and his mom just went with it.

Then it was time for the piñata. Why haven't these stupid things been outlawed? They never break apart, the kids start crying and Dad just winds up pulling the Tootsie Rolls out of the donkey's ass and throwing them on the floor. Or in this case, a Mountain Gorilla's ass.

I looked at all the other adults checking their watches. Why were we here? For the kids? They too appeared to be barely tolerating this penance. My kids look happier when I tell them to make their beds and get dressed for church.

What does all this mean? Childhood is supposed to involve a great deal of Fun, after all. But advertisers know this and marketing to children is an ever-growing niche. We are sucking up this crap as fast as the market can spew it out. We're teaching kids that Fun is an item in a box. And that it's somehow better if it costs more.

It's also better if we can control the Fun to make sure it's safe and educational to boot. Boy, I sure loved those educational toys when I was a kid. Didn't you?

Happy Birthday, **Connor**! Are you having Fun yet? He looked completely overwhelmed by all the fuss. His hovering parents were trying to make sure **Connor** behaved and impressed his grandparents and his friends' parents. Poor kid. Why do I have the feeling **Connor** is going to have an intense dislike of mountain gorillas when he's an adult, but won't be able to figure out quite why?

The Politics of the Playgroup

The playgroup is the new mother's salvation. Whatever its faults, a playgroup offers new moms one of the few opportunities to meet other new moms. This is the first chance to compare/contrast your kid with others, and to determine how badly you're fucking up. You get to see that you're not alone in your feelings of loneliness, despair and budding alcoholism. You get to hone the newly developing skills you'll need later in your parenting career, like putting up with other people's kids.

After all, it's really all about you. Everyone knows that the babies don't really play at this age. They just sit on the floor and drool. The Books call this Parallel Play.

So ditch the kids in the sunroom while you and your new cronies drink coffee and bitch. The talk is lightening fast, and no one really listens to anyone else. After all, this is the only time all week you have to talk to other adults. Make the most of it.

When you're searching out a playgroup, it helps to find other moms with similar interests. If you're the granola and birkenstock type, run far away from the manicured Neiman Marcus set. This may seem an obvious point, but new mothers are so desperate for company it's not unusual to see a Wiccan mom and a CCD teacher mom making nice at the playground. Or a Vegan and a Perdue Chicken heiress borrowing Huggies from each other.

But, that said, any playgroup is better than none. You never know who you'll meet or with whom you'll hit it off. I've always found it interesting how I became friends with women I never would have considered approaching just because we happened to get knocked up around the same time.

I was lucky. Our playgroup got along pretty well even though we were all vastly different. Who knew a Celine Dion fan could make nice with a Nick Cave devotee? Just goes to show you how strong is the bond of motherhood.

We would mostly chat about the same things. We would bring up our concerns of the moment, worrying about the various developmental milestones on which our children had fallen short, and then we would all reassure each other that everything will be just fine. The marriage/in-law subject never failed to provide an interesting diversion. And I knew more about these women's obstetrical histories than anyone had a right to know. The key was: keep it light. If anyone ever revealed any true emotion, any depth, the rest would shuffle nervously. Hey, this is supposed to be fun. Tell it to your shrink, lady.

After awhile you may run out of things to talk about, but do not despair. It's just a signal to throw some new life into the conversation. Everyone's tired of trashing their husbands and talking about weight loss. So here are some ideas guaranteed to help spark animated, lively discussion:

Velveeta or Kraft singles: How does one choose?

Is Thomas really a cheeky little engine or is he just an asshole?

Compare and contrast: Pop-Tarts frosted vs. unfrosted.

How much of your kids' Halloween candy are you allowed to steal before you're officially a thieving scumbag?

Things Disney owns that you had no idea about and have been unknowingly supporting.

Thinking outside the john: The best places to hide from your kids.

If you could assassinate one character from a children's show, who would it be? Baby Bop? Scrappy Doo? Use your imagination.

Extra credit for cruel and unusual punishment.

What's the deal with Precious Moments and Boyd's Bears collectibles anyway? Are they serious? And is Thomas Kinkade really the Painter of Light®?

What percentage of the ten vitamins and iron has your kid consumed if she's only eaten the marshmallows out of the Lucky Charms?

In a steel cage match, who would win: the A&D's or the Desitin's?

What's the longest you've gone in the winter without shaving your legs? How about the pits? Come on, fess up.

Even if you find something new to talk about, after awhile the playgroup will begin to fall apart. New babies arrive and complicate schedules. Discussing the play-by-play details of everyone's labors and deliveries no longer sounds like interesting conversation. Older kids start school and form new friendships. Fighting with your kids about their homework now takes hours out of every day.

The moms from the playgroup who were thrown together have by now realized that some of the friendships formed were of the moment only. A few, at best, will develop into lifelong closeness.

The end of the playgroup days are bittersweet. Gone are the mornings where you have nothing else to do but drink coffee in a sunlit living room. Gone are the days when your schedule revolved around naptimes. You start to think about the next stage in life and new activities you want to pursue, such as trying to find your missing waistline. You suddenly notice those enticing things on the shelf with covers and pages. You begin to want some time to yourself. Intrusions into your new, hard-won freedom seem more and more annoying.

So bye-bye playgroups. You were sweet. I'm out in the world again now, but I might not be saying that if it weren't for those chatty, caffeinated mornings watching a gaggle of toddlers barf on the Megablocks. They got me though. If I ever bemoan my insanely busy days I remind myself of those lonely mornings when I would put out the coffee and muffins and keep checking out the window, hoping at least one of the moms would show up.

Dieting the Mommy Way

Atkins, South Beach, Jenny Craig, Weight Watchers and The Zone have all come and gone, but it's too hard to stick to a diet now that my cooking amounts to heating up chicken nuggets. What to do?

I've come up with my own diet, one that all mothers can follow easily. It's called the "Are You Finished With That?" Diet.

If you stick to this one, it'll really work. It's all about portion control and suppression of appetite. The trick is to eat the kid's leftovers only. Are you ready? Sure you are. Chances are the first meal is already prepared and spilled all over the table. Here goes.

Day One:

Breakfast:

- Leftover rice cereal mixed with breast milk. Eat it before it gets partially digested and watery from your baby's saliva.
- Half a jar of Gerber peaches. Hmm, not bad.
- Bowl of Dinosaur Eggs oatmeal that your son begged for then refused to touch.
- Any wayward Cheerios you happen to spot before they get stepped on.

Lunch:

- Two spoonfuls of cold mac and cheese.
- Bread crust from a PBJ.
- Warm Nestle Quik.

Snack:

- Whatever came home in the lunch box uneaten. Today it's half a box of raisins and an unwrapped cheese stick garnished with teeth marks .

Cocktail hour:
• Giant martini with extra olives. Shaken, stirred, who cares?

Dinner:
• Slice of pepperoni you stole from kid's pizza.
• Three blackened french fries. Scrape them off the cookie sheet.
• The grapes that were a little too mushy for the Princess to eat.

Dessert:
• Halloween/Easter/Valentine candy, in season.

That's an average day on the "Are You Finished With That?" diet. It's easy. No special food preparation or complicated shopping lists.

Some more ideas:
• Cubes of carrots left in the bowl after your kids eat the chicken noodle soup.
• Jar of Stage Three baby food lasagne rescued just before the expiration date. (The kid moved on to finger foods before it could be eaten.)
• Remainder of the SpongeBob sherbet pop that your son put in the freezer for later but forgot.
• Half a frozen Go-Gurt
• Smoothie: Combine remains from dinnertime milk glasses and the bruised bits you cut from a banana that your Precious wouldn't touch. Blend.

- Strawberry ice cream from the Neopolitan box, since the chocolate and vanilla were eaten last Memorial Day. Flick off the ice crystals and freezer burn.

Try these handy recipes when it's time to entertain:

Party Mix:
Combine the stale remains from the boxes of cereal you've been saving. A nice choice is the Lucky Charms/Honey Nut Cheerio combo, sans marshmallows of course. They're long gone.

Juice Box Daiquiris:
Remove straws from half-finished juice boxes after child's birthday party. Squeeze leftover juice into blender. Add ice and enough rum or other alcohol to kill all the germs in the juice. Blend.

Pot Luck Crudite Platter:
Remember when you were inspired by that "Fun Foods Kids Will Love" article and you bought black olives for pizza faces and celery for ants on a log? Look in the pantry. Betcha the black olives are still in there. Remember: Anything looks better with a toothpick stuck in it and placed on a "Happy Birthday Four-Year-Old" party napkin.

Well, that's the plan. You get the idea. Just eat whatever's left when the kids leave the table. Guaranteed to kill your appetite more effectively than mainlining Ephedra. Think how sleek you'll look this summer. You'd better order your Land's End Tankini a size smaller!

I'll Get You, My Pretty

Are you a good witch or a bad witch? Maybe I'm tempting an intellectual property-infringement lawsuit by quoting that line, but it seems to fit in this case. You're a mom, ergo a witch, but just how bad are you?

All moms have their good moments. We also have our witchy, satanic moments that make us cringe when remembered. Hell, after a few years of working on the chain gang even Penelope Leach is going to be looking around nervously, waiting for a house to fall on her.

Track your inevitable death spiral from "Disinfect The Pacifier" mom to "Just Play The Damn Nintendo And Leave Me Alone" mom with this handy quiz. Keep track of your answers and see just how far down the yellow brick road you've progressed.

1. Your pre-schooler has just received another birthday party invite to Chuck E. Cheese's. The party will take place from 1-3:30 on a Saturday, thereby blowing the whole day. What do you do?

A. Respond immediately saying your child would love to come, and by the way what would little Brandon/Braden/Brendan like for his birthday present?

B. Hide the invite from your kid and hope no one mentions it in his class.

C. Punch a hole in the wall.

2. Your child's school district has sent home a complicated flyer explaining the new reading curriculum. What do you do?

A. Read it and attend the open mike discussion forum at the next Board of Ed meeting. Go online and research the test results of other districts using this curriculum so you'll be ready for a healthy debate.

B. Attempt to read it but become confused and frustrated after the fourteenth pie chart outlining the Phonics vs. Whole Language debate.

C. Figure that if your kid is reading then the school must be doing something right. Mix yourself a cocktail.

3. Halloween is looming and all the other moms are making their kids' costumes. What do you do?

A. Buy the furry fabric and the Simplicity pattern and vow to make the best Scrappy Doo costume that L'il Learners Preschool has ever seen. That'll show that bitchy mom who always sends her kid to school in ironed jeans. She thinks she's so great!

B. Draw some stripes on your kids sweatpants. Wrap a bent coat hanger with Saran Wrap and duct tape it to your kid's back. Voila! Instant bumblebee!

C. Tape a toilet paper core to her forehead and make her go as a unicorn.

4. Bake Sale time! The school is raising money for the fourth grade's field trip to the waste treatment plant and they need your help. What do you do?

A. Bake spelt flour/raisin cookies and deliver them in a hand-decorated tin with beads spelling out the name of school.

B. Buy the slice and bake dough tube and frost with store brand canned frosting. Screw it, that's good enough.

C. Stand for fifteen minutes in the bakery department of the supermarket, trying to decide which cookies can pass as homemade.

5. An article about the horrors of choking possibilities freaks you out. What steps do you take to avoid a potential catastrophe?

A. Hire a babyproofer to sweep the dangers from your home so you can sleep at night. Take an infant CPR course at the adult school. Cut each grape into 24 pieces.

B. Make the kid eat every meal standing on his head.

C. Cross your fingers and hope the kid makes it to his fifth birthday.

6. Some states now mandate that a child should ride in a car seat until he weighs eighty pounds. How do you feel about this?

A. "Car seats bring peace of mind. I attended a clinic at the local police station where they made sure our car seat was installed properly."

B. "I hate lugging it around but it beats going to the gym. My arms have never looked more toned."

C. "Eighty pounds? Oh come on. Does this mean Calista Flockhart and her son have matching car seats?"

7. It's time for the annual Holiday Concert at your kid's school. How do you plan to enjoy this event?

A. Get there early, record every precious detail on the camcorder from the front row. Weep when they sing "Jingle Bell Rock" for some reason. Maybe it's time for an adjustment to your medication.

B. Arrive late and stand through the unintelligible kindergarten salute to Kwaanza. Find the nearest exit like you're studying the safety card in a Boeing 737. Keep in mind that the nearest exit may be behind you.

C. Figure that if your kid is in third grade, you can be a half hour late and still arrive in time to catch his class's performance of "Dreidel Dreidel." Leave immediately after, pleading stomach flu. Watch the crowds part!

8. Your kid needs new shoes. What do you do?

A. Take out a second mortgage and go to Stride Rite where you can be sure to have your child's feet properly sized. Rest assured that by doing this you've avoided turning your kid's feet into twisted clubs, and that you have not ruined his chances for a track scholarship to Princeton.

B. Go to Payless, buy a half size up from the old ones, stick your thumb on his toe to check the fit as if you know what you're doing. Pick up some cool boots for yourself while you're at it. Like those over there. Hey, they're not half bad! Who's going to know? Fifteen bucks? Done!

C. Dig in the closet for your older kid's hand-me-downs. Cover up scuffs with a Sharpie.

9. Horrors! Your child has discovered his privates and can't leave 'em alone. Now what?

A. Go online and find all the "facts of life" books on Amazon. Check the reviews and get the best one. Read it with your child and explain the proper names of those parts of the body and what their functions are. Ask him if he has any questions.

B. Tell him what he's doing is perfectly natural, but if he wants to do it he has to go to his room and be alone. Then go pour a glass of wine and wonder if you've just turned him into a compulsive masturbator.

C. Say to him: "For crying out loud get your hands out of your pants and give your wingdizzler a rest already."

10. Your child is going through yet another bout of "separation anxiety." You and your husband have tickets to a show you've waited months to see, but your child is sobbing hysterically and humping your leg as you try to leave. What do you do?

A. Have your husband drive the babysitter home and comfort little bunnykins. After all, she won't need you like this forever. Isn't it nice that she loves you so?

B. Go to the show anyway but refuse to enjoy it. Give the babysitter a big tip and vow never to go out again until the kid is in high school.

C. Sneak out when your kid isn't looking and have the time of your life.

Now, let's take a look at your answers. If you answered A to most questions you are a very good mother and an example to us all. Now please go and insert that massive suppository you so desperately need. If you answered B to most questions you're on the path to bad motherhood, but you still have a long way to go. A few more years of trying to keep up the charade should wear you down. If you answered C to most questions, you've surrendered, Dorothy.

How To Be Friends With Working Moms: A Primer

I have a lot of friends who are wonderful mothers who freely admit that staying home would make them crazy. I never know quite how to respond. They look at me and I know they are thinking "how the hell does she do it? *Why* the hell does she do it?"

Hmmm.

To this I say: Of *course* it makes you crazy. That's the bloody point. All you have to do is make eye contact with another mom who's going through it and you know you're looking at a soulmate, a member of the club of warrior women.

Some of us stay-at-homes secretly feel that if you're not at home questioning your sanity and every life choice you've made to date it's just not fair. You shouldn't get to be a mother without feeling crazy. Without feeling bored, frustrated, overmedicated and like you've given up on yourself.

Besides, if you're not being driven crazy by motherhood then how can you possibly fulfill its most basic tenet: passing your neuroses onto your children? It's a mother's sacred duty. If we don't have any mental illnesses ourselves, how can our children inherit?

It's the craziness you get from your mom which makes the world go 'round. Think about it. The world would be lacking most of its great literature if the authors had had sane mothers. Not to mention that the entire fields of psychiatry, ice-cream manufacturing and pharmacology would collapse as well. So you're doing the world a favor by staying home with your kids. Think of it that way.

I say it's no fair that you get to go to work and have a jolly old time all day talking to adults who don't spit food at you. You have the paid help break up the fights between your kids and negotiate whose turn it is to be Luigi and whose turn it is to be Mario, then you waltz in at 7pm and have the kids actually happy to see you. You do your fifteen minute quality-time requirement and you're done. No fucking fair! It's like the guy who ran the New York marathon by ducking into a subway in Brooklyn and emerging near the Central Park finish line.

Yeah, I know this is a gross oversimplification. I know that working moms will be outraged at this callous treatment of their busy lives. But hey, I speak for the stay-at-homes who have heard themselves referred to as the "muffia" by working mothers who suppose we do nothing but bake muffins all day. So cry me a river, Ms. Have-It-All.

Hey, calm down. I'm kidding. This whole working vs. stay-at-home motherhood comparison has grown tiresome. Every mother I know who is home for now used to work and will again. A lot of moms who are working full-time now are thinking about cutting back their hours or stopping entirely. It's a fluid thing.

Maybe we should band together and start a revolution! Fight against our culture of materialism that keeps us on the treadmill! Fight against the corporate mentality that crushes any human need in its path! If you get anywhere with this, let me know.

Meanwhile, I'm going to stay the course because I really have no choice at the moment. Maybe the craziness will lead me to some higher mental place. I'm still hoping. I glimpse nirvana occasionally, like the one time my son opened a granola bar wrapper all by himself and I was there to witness it.

Occasionally the workies will slip here and there. The P.C. guard will be dropped. One of my working friends mentioned a mutual acquaintance who decided to stay home with her kids.

The conversation went a little something like this:

"Can you see Ann as a STAY-AT-HOME MOTHER?"

"Well, yes, I can. Why not?"

It's amusing to see the backpedaling commence.

"Oh, well, I mean, it's just that she's so smart ... "

"Meaning?"

"Umm...hey look over there! Nordstrom's is having a shoe sale!"

Ohhhhkay. So how do us stay-at-home freaks deal with this? You still like your friend and want to remain loyal, even if she does have a nice manicure, hair that has been brushed recently and a savings account.

The temptation is to give her a guilt trip. You want to describe all the enriching experiences you have had with your kids. Play up the fact that you dropped off the forgotten lunchbox at school and how happy your child was that you were there for him. Describe the wonderful hours whiled away at the library reading *Go, Dog, Go.* Just don't mention the scolding you gave your kid for forgetting his lunch, thereby blowing the tender moment, or that you had to pull your hysterical child out of the library after you were asked to leave.

But anyway that guilt-trip induction technique is small minded. Don't stoop to that level, no matter how tempting. Remember, your friend thinks about things like meetings, PDA's and business lunches, so you have to speak her language. Playgroups can be renamed status meetings, a PTA bake sale can become a business lunch, if you grab an oatmeal muffin and eat it on the spot. Go ahead and get a Palm Pilot if it helps and you don't mind looking like a supreme dork in front of the other stay-at-homes.

One mother I know actually had business cards printed. Her title? Mother of Susannah and Jordan. (Yes, some of us are that desperate for respect.) Be creative. Your working friend's ears will perk up and she will actually listen to you with the respect paid to a functioning member of society, rather than a curious object of pity.

One technique that really hurts no one, except your own mortal soul, is to shamelessly engage in schadenfreude. When she complains that her kid is angry and having trouble socially because he resents the time his mother spends at work, quietly gloat. Enjoy your feelings of mothering superiority. Never mind that your own kids are just as fucked up and you have no one to blame but yourself.

Also, beware the parenting gods. Judge not other mothers lest you too be judged and smited. Or smote. Whatever. There will be a plague upon your house. You know I'm talking about: Strep Throat striking on a Sunday Morn, six-foot snow drifts and a broken DVD player.

Instead, try pretending you are a working woman who occasionally uses her brain for something other than sniffing her toddler's butt to ascertain if he took a dump or just farted. Drop the kids off with a neighbor for a few hours. Go home, shower and shave your legs. Lose the toothpaste-stained tee shirt and put on grown-up clothes. Ride the train into the city carrying a vat of Starbucks and a *New York Times.* Look at your watch a lot and speak into your cell phone. *"No, that won't work. It's a crazy week. I've got deadlines up the wazoo."* Notice the dead eyes of the beaten commuters around you and ask yourself if this is what you really want after all. When everyone else gets off the train in the city just turn around and ride back home. Maybe you'll feel better.

If nothing else works, remind yourself that staying at home with your children is just a passing stage. It's hard to believe now but the rest of your life really does not resemble the classic perspective lesson. You know, the one with the vanishing point on the horizon and nothing but emptiness and hopelessness ahead. There really will be a time when Edvard Munch's *The Scream* no longer feels so familiar. Try to believe it when old-timers tell you that kids grow up so fast. After all, it's hard to believe your baby is five years old already. Hasn't the time just flown by? Doesn't it seem like, well, five years ago that he was born?

So for what it's worth we will be able to look back and say we were there for our kids. We saw it all. The first steps, the smiles at school pickup time, the warm cuddliness of their bodies after nap. Even though it made us crazy we were present, unless we count the hours we spent hiding from them in the john and sobbing.

Literature for Marginalized Mothers

The Pleasantville Adult School Catalog
Sign up today! Classes now meet at the Middle School since that unfortunate plumbing incident at the VFW hall.

Course Number 123: Continuing the "Literature for Marginalized Mothers" series, this semester we are offering "The Classic American Short Story." Here is a quick synopsis of the stories we will be covering:

The Lottery by Shirley Jackson
Everyone gathers around the preschool on that late spring morning. Moms wander in, some fresh from the video store/dry cleaner/supermarket rounds. Every year they gather, exchanging everyday small talk. They all know what will happen; none think they may be the unlucky one. The circle tightens. A name is pulled from the hat. The preschool teacher reads it: Nancy Wilkens. All turn to stare at Nancy as she shrieks in disbelief. "NOOOO! It can't be me. There must be some mistake! Pull out another name!" All the other mothers regard Nancy with silent contempt. They shuffle back to their minivans, their station wagons, their SUVs. Nancy is left alone at the preschool wailing and screaming at her fate. Yes, this year, it's Nancy's name that was drawn. It's her turn to buy the munchkins for the class holiday party.

Occurrence at Owl Creek Bridge by Ambrose Bierce
She is standing on the bridge. The Windstar has a flat tire and she is faced with the prospect of changing the tire herself because she absent-mindedly let the AAA lapse. She is feeling overwhelmed by horror at this turn of events. How did she get here? Is it all a

dream? She thinks: are those really my ghastly children in the car, fighting over the only Gameboy that still has working batteries? She looks down into the swirling river and suddenly she jumps in, escaping her fate. From under the cool water she can hear her kids whining, but as she swims she leaves them further and further behind. She is free! Crawling out of the river many miles downstream, she begins to stumble through a long, peaceful glade. On through the forest she walks, then runs. Something wonderful is waiting for her. It's coming into focus now. What is it? It's ... a man! Yes, it's that Viggo guy from *Lord of the Rings,* waiting for her with open arms. She runs towards him with abandon. *SLAM!* She is suddenly snapped back to reality by the sound of a car door closing. Her little boy has gotten out of the car and is peeing off the bridge into the churning water below.

To Build a Fire by Jack London

Her husband was working late again, and as she watched the snow pile up she knew she would have to shovel it. She located the one snow shovel without a broken handle behind the overloaded recycling bins. She even found the Winnie the Pooh kiddie shovel in the crawlspace. Out she went into the bitter cold. Soon she realized her shovel was the heavy one that snow always stuck to. Why didn't she go to Home Depot to get a decent one when the snow was first forecast? She began to feel colder and colder. The dog slunk at her heels, sensing her despair. A fire! That's what was needed! The thought of a crackling fire kept her going. Shoveling complete, she went right to the fireplace with newspaper and matches. The dog watched excitedly. She struck a match, and the newspaper burned beautifully. But the Duraflame just wouldn't catch. Shivering, slumping in defeat, hands black from newspaper ink, she gave up. The dog approached her apprehensively, sensing the end was near. He sniffed her feet and then padded away.

The Legend of Sleepy Hollow by Washington Irving
The Sleepy Hollow Charter School was buzzing about the upcoming Halloween party. Most of the gossip involved a woman legendary in her ability to extort volunteer hours out of the even most reluctant parents. All of the moms were a little afraid of her, for it was said that she haunted hapless mothers with endless phone calls if her efforts to recruit class trip drivers went unrewarded. Her name was Heddy. Finally the big party day arrived. Just as the children sat down to enjoy their carob-chip, gluten-free cookies, Heddy saw it. The big bowl of peanut M&M's. "WHO BROUGHT THESE PEANUT M&M's INTO THIS NUT-FREE ENVIRONMENT?" Heddy thundered. All the moms quaked in their Nordstrom booties until one mom came forward. "I did, Heddy. I wasn't aware of the No Nuts rule. Sorry." Heddy was not satisfied. After the party the unsuspecting mother drove home, only to realize Heddy was following her in a huge, black Ford Expedition. The last thing she saw was a huge pumpkin hurtling towards her head. The next day she didn't show up at school. There were rumors of foul play, but no one ever challenged Heddy again, and Sleepy Hollow Charter School remains a safe, nut-free learning place to this day.

The Cask of Amontillado by Edgar Allen Poe
Tonight was the night: my first evening away from the house and kids in months. My husband was due home from work soon to take over. I made sure the jammies were on the bed so my husband wouldn't dress them in Hefty bags, claiming it was all he

could find. Finally I heard the door open. He was home! I ran downstairs, so happy was I to see him and to know that my hour of delivery was close at hand. I ran through the details of the evening. "Are you sure you can manage?" I asked. "I could get the babysitter to come and help…you seem so tired." "Nonsense! I can do this! Show me where the kids are." "Follow me" I said. Through the twisted catacombs of the back hall we stumbled, bruising our feet in the gloom on stray K'NEX pieces and wooden blocks. Finally, we reach the niche we call a playroom. All the kids were there, each engrossed in their own dark pursuit. He looked around, a little stunned, as I began to back away. "Well, have a good night," I said. "I'll be home late, don't wait up." He suddenly looked panicked. "Wait…where are you going?" "Just to the movies with the Amontillado's. You'll be fine." I backed away further. The kids approached him and locked him up in their embrace. He struggled to break free. The kids said, "Come on, Daddy, play Mousetrap with us!" As I closed the door behind me I heard him scream.

The Celebrated Jumping Frog of Calaveras County by Mark Twain
Calaveras County Elementary School's first grade has a class pet, a huge bullfrog named Jumpy. Every weekend the children take turns bringing Jumpy home. This Friday it's the Webster family's turn. The whole family is very excited. Everyone, that is, except Mrs. Webster. This is because Jumpy has to be fed live crickets. As if that isn't bad enough, Mrs. Webster is forced to drive to three different pet stores to find the right ones. Finally returning home, she finds Jumpy has escaped from the cage. She searches frantically, thinking he could be anywhere. Suddenly she sees her toddler sitting in the playroom with Jumpy on her lap. "Don't move!"

shouts Mrs. Webster. "We don't want to scare him off!" She approaches Jumpy slowly, but Jumpy just sits there. She realizes that the toddler has fed Jumpy all the marbles from the marble maze game. Not only is Jumpy not jumping, but he's also looking a little ill. Back into the car she goes, hoping the pet store will have a bullfrog that will pass for Jumpy on Monday morning.

Hey Mom, What's In Your Stars?

Today's horoscope by Skye Stargazer, noted astrologer and mother of five.

Aries (Mar 21-Apr 20): Resist the urge to form a posse to beat up the mother who brings in California rolls for preschool snack. Her pathological need to show off is not your concern; just have pity on her. Don't forget you promised to make cookies for the bake sale tomorrow. See if your neighbor has any vanilla extract now so you won't be knocking on the A&P's door at midnight like you did last year. Lucky number: 1 teaspoon

Taurus (Apr 21-May21): The wishbone on your kitchen windowsill is finally dry enough for your kids to fight over. Pluto in your chart means it's belt-tightening time. Take back the CVS circular from under the guinea pig cage and you might be able to rescue a coupon for a twelve-pack of paper towels. On the other hand, Pluto could mean you'll be dragging the kids to DisneyWorld come spring break. Hope for the former. Lucky number: 5 Days/4 Nights

Gemini (May 22-June 21): You should have known you'd be shunned by the rest of the mothers for allowing your child to play with a *water gun.* And in the future ask if your child's friend is allergic to pine nuts before you let them make pesto in the Easy-Bake oven. Next time, consider having a lawyer draw up document that waives the child's parents' right to sue. Really, you should be more careful. Lucky number: $50,000 Out-of-Court Settlement

Cancer (Jun 22-July 22): Just because you're on your hands and knees looking for the Lego Race Car Driver's tiny plastic helmet does not mean you'll be doing this the rest of your life. Keep the big picture in mind. This perspective will help you sit through the fifth grade viola recital as well. Try this mantra: Every Good Boy Deserves Fudge. Venus in your chart means it's time to ditch the nursing bras since you stopped nursing three years ago. Head over to Target for some new ones already. Lucky number: 36B

Leo (Jul 23-Aug 22): The moon figures strongly, making it likely your kid will drop his pants again today in Kindergarten. Also, he's back to eating paste. Prepare for a phone call from the teacher. A question about vaginas from your third-grader might mean it's time for The Talk. Start rehearsing nervously now. And believe it or not your preschooler really will be potty-trained someday. If you buy a gross of Pull-Ups at CostCo that just might do the trick. Lucky numbers: 1 and 2.

Virgo (Aug 23-Sep 23): Romance appears strong for you today. Your partner will come home with flowers and that special look in his eye. There's no getting around it: you're going to have to give it up. If he's really desperate you may be able to get him to do the bath routine and storytime too. Maybe you can talk him into a quickie; you'll be done in time for *The Daily Show*. Lucky number: 69

Libra (Sep 24-Oct 23): The struggles you have had lately with your in-laws will ease once you make that move to Wellington, New Zealand. The stars say you will find true love, but you might have to settle for gawking at that hunky barista in Starbucks. Watch out for the chicken nuggets in the microwave. Last time you forgot they were in there and they exploded. Lucky number: 325°

Scorpio (Oct 24-Nov 22): It's not your imagination. Those really are fruit flies. Your child must have stashed an apple core somewhere. Good luck finding it. Mercury figures prominently, so beware of car problems. You put off that oil change too long last time around and were stranded at Mommy and Me when the car wouldn't start, remember? Get your butt over to Jiffy Lube today. Lucky number: 10W-40

Sagittarius (Nov 23-Dec 21): Take a positive step towards more assertive behavior and cancel your subscription to *Perfect Parent* magazine. A wedding invitation arrives, giving you the opportunity to dress up for the first time in years. Don't panic. You've got three months to lose the weight and find something to wear. If that doesn't work, there's a sale at Ann Taylor Woman. Lucky number: 20 percent off.

Capricorn (Dec 22-Jan 20): Just because you're thinking about having another child doesn't mean you actually have to. There's a big difference between fantasy and reality, sister. Resist the temptation to go straight back to bed this morning. Keep your eye on the prize: in an hour your kids will be in school and you can have some goddamned coffee in peace. I won't mention that you'll soon be driving to school to deliver a forgotten math textbook. Lucky number: π

Aquarius (Jan 21-Feb 19): Time to simplify: clean your kids' playroom and you'll find brand new toys that are perfect for regifting. Deal with the stack of school flyers on the counter you've been avoiding or risk getting lumped in with the "loser moms" who don't return permission slips. You may have to hide in your home all next week to avoid attending that Pampered Chef party, but it's totally worth it. On second thought, just go to the damn party. You need kitchen gadgets and you need them right now. Lucky number: 1/2 cup.

Pisces (Feb 20-Mar 20): It's not worth keeping up the perfect mom charade if you're strung out on Xanax and Nestle's Crunch.

Arrange more "away" playdates and stop being a martyr. For God's sake give the scrapbook a rest. Your fingers are permanently glued together and you've developed facial tics. Get acquainted with the concept of a babysitter. It's cheaper than therapy. Lucky number: 7 bucks an hour.

If your birthday is today: Chances are you've not had a minute to think about it until your husband says he's taking you out to dinner. Scramble to find another babysitter since your old one has a boyfriend now. You won't kiss your kids goodnight for fear of messing up your lipstick and you'll feel guilty about it the whole evening. Go ahead and have dessert. Fuck South Beach, it's your birthday.

Keeping It Real

Reality TV is just too contrived. Why drag people to Belize and make them eat tarantulas when the real horror and human drama is as close as your frozen food section? Let's have some REAL reality shows. For instance:

Survivor: Route 80

The *Kids Bop 5* CD will be played on a continuous loop as the mothers drive their children cross country. The last mother who does not purposely rear-end a gasoline tanker truck or drive off a bridge in Madison County wins.

Fear Factor

Contestants vie for bragging rights by facing three horrifying tasks. They are:

1. Changing a diaper after a corn/raisin/Cefzil blowout.
2. Wearing a butt-floss string bikini to the town pool on a crowded Saturday afternoon.
3. Borrowing four car seats, installing them in a rickety 1988 Volvo wagon, driving five three-year olds to a community theatre performance of *The Hobbit* and sitting through the entire show.

The winner gets a lifetime supply of Purel, a sarong from Target and the chance to take an ax to the car seats.

I'm a Celebrity Mom! Get Me Out of Here!

Ten A-list celeb moms go shoe shopping with their kids at Payless, pack their own kids' lunches and bring their kids to Sears Portrait

Studio for the annual Christmas portrait with no help from assistants or nannies. Hilarity ensues. The first to complete all the tasks with out resorting to Vicodin or the Kabbalah wins. The winner gets nothing, just like regular moms.

The Mole

One of the women in the Tuesday morning playgroup is not a mother after all. See if she can fool the other mothers before she blows her cover and all hell breaks loose. Tonight: the other mothers become suspicious when the Mole asks for decaf!

Manor House

Watch a group of trailer park moms try to pass themselves as members of the Hamptons horsy set. Best episode: Jeannie Mae hides her hillbilly drawl with a passable Long Island Lockjaw, but gives herself away when she asks where the "shitter" is.

The Simple Life

Park Avenue mothers have to live on a normal budget. Tonight they have only $25.00 to buy groceries for the week. Watch the hijinks as they are introduced to family pack ground beef, oatmeal and the concept of "price per unit." Best episode: Bitsy and Muffy come to blows over the last pair of marked down Jeff Gordon NASCAR slippers in Wal-Mart.

Queer Eye for the Frumpy Mom

The Fab Five take on their biggest challenge: finding *fabulous* baby-proof covering for the Eames chair. Watch Carson have a stroke as he rifles through mom's underwear drawer and finds yellowed nursing bras, even though the baby is seven.

1900 House

Mothers and their children have to live in an authentically recreated circa 1900 home with no modern conveniences whatsoever. Tonight: See a corseted Mom happily deal with diphtheria and typhus. *Happily?* Yes indeed, for anything beats hearing that damned *Bob The Builder* theme one more time.

American Idol Worship

Mothers try to talk their kids out of craving brand-name crap like Nike and McDonald's by exposing the manipulative evil of big business. Any mother who manages to keep her kid's eyes from glazing over for at least thirty seconds wins. Winning mothers will receive a new wardrobe from the Gap. a week at Epcot and a Gateway PC with a Pentium processor.

The Real World

Six mothers leave their families and have to learn to live together in a painfully hip loft, sharing martinis and gossip. Unfortunately the show was cancelled when the mothers had so much fun that they wouldn't leave the loft and go home. Look for the sequel: "The Real World 2," or, "The Kids Are Here Looking For Us! Hide!"

I'M DONE! I'M DONE!

Long ago I reached the stage I once feared: I know I will not have any more babies. When I was a young mother I thought getting to that point would be heartbreakingly sad.

But the realization I once thought would bring on paroxysms of tears and glass-shattering keening has turned out to be a breath of fresh air. It's a gift. The awareness that life goes in stages, and that's not such a bad thing, is priceless. I'm done, SO done, with babies and all that surrounds them and I couldn't be happier.

Not that I didn't love my babies! No little cherubs were more chewed upon for their deliciousness, no sweethearts were more cuddled, kissed, and fussed over. I actually loved being pregnant, when I wasn't feeling like shit, and was in awe of the changes my body was going through. I didn't even have to think about it, my body just knew what to do. That wondrous knowledge made me feel linked with women the world over. OK, that's the disclaimer.

But I also remember the all-encompassing worry and care these new little ones demanded. The knee-shaking fatigue, bleeding nipples, stitched-up crotch. And that's just the physical side-effects.

I remember bursting into hormone-enhanced tears as I ventured out for the first time, my first newborn in his new pram, and noticed a big group of unencumbered singles partying and laughing. I felt so alone, my body was aching, and for that moment I thought my life was over.

The complete loss of freedom, spontaneity and time for creativity stifled me and crushed the light in me for years. I wasn't aware how much I had sacrificed until I began to come out from under it. My children began to get bigger. One day all three played with each other, without needing me. I began to actually enjoy my kids, in addition to loving them.

Freedom comes in little bits. The first one off to preschool, the second one suddenly in school full-time, the third one is registered for kindergarten. The oldest gets his first cell phone and tells you he's going out after school with his friends. A little more freedom is handed to you, so slowly it's anti-climactic. You don't realize how far you have come.

Not until you see a pregnant mom pushing a double stroller, looking a little shell-shocked and distracted. That was you once, and you suddenly remember every nuance of it. And you don't think, oh, those were the days! It was so nice! No, instead every neuron of your brain screams "How did I do it? THANK GOD I made it through those days." That's when you know you're done.

Feels good, doesn't it? We did it.

Publishing the Works of Extraordinary Mom Writers

Wyatt-MacKenzie Publishing, Inc

WyMacPublishing.com